MW01700761

The Muse Strikes Back

HUMAN SCIENCES MONOGRAPH SERIES

The Human Sciences Monograph Series is a Canadian bilingual publication which stresses the interconnections between theory, practice, and pedagogy in the studies conducted in Humanities and Social Sciences. It provides scholars working across these fields with an accessible way to share their thinking and thus foster a healthy conversation about the implications of the day-to-day work they do within the Humanities and Social Sciences in the contemporary Canadian university.

Address: Human Sciences Monograph Series, R.D. Parker Building, Laurentian University, Sudbury, Ontario, P3E 2C6 ; FAX: (705) 675-4885.

Managing Editor: Ali Reguigui, Departernent of French Studies and Translation, Laurentian University.

Editorial Advisory Board: Ronald B. Bond (University of Calgary), William Francis Mackey, FRSC. (CIRAL : Laval University), Igor Mel'čuk (University of Montreal), Anthony Paré (McGill University).

SÉRIE MONOGRAPHIQUE EN SCIENCES HUMAINES

La Série monographique en sciences humaines est une publication canadienne bilingue qui met l'accent sur les rapports entre la théorie, la pratique et la pédagogie dans les recherches menées en Sciences humaines et sociales. Elle offre aux universitaires qui ouvrent dans ces domaines un moyen de partager le fruit de leurs réflexions et encourage ainsi un échange utile au sujet de leur travail quotidien au sein des Sciences humaines et sociales dans l'université canadienne moderne

Adresse: Série monographique en sciences humaines, Edifice R. D. Parker, Université Laurentienne, Sudbury (Ontario), P3E 2C6; Télécopieur : (705) 675-4885.

Directeur : Ali Reguigui, Département d'études françaises et de traduction, Université Laurentienne.

Comité Consultatif: Ronald B. Bond (Université de Calgary), William Francis Mackey, FRSC. (CIRAL : Université Laval), Igor Mel'čuk (Université de Montréal), Anthony Paré (Université McGill).

The Muse Strikes Back

Female Narratology in the Novels of Hédi Bouraoui

by

Elizabeth Sabiston

Library and Archives Canada Cataloguing in Publication

Sabiston, Elizabeth Jean, 1937-
The muse strikes back : female narratology in the novels of Hédi Bouraoui / by Elizabeth Jean Sabiston.

(Human sciences monograph series ; 9)
Includes bibliographical references.
ISBN 0-88667-059-4

1. Bouraoui, Hédi, 1932- – Criticism and interpretation. 2. Bouraoui, Hédi, 1932- – Characters – Women. 3. Narration (Rhetoric) I. Title. II. Series.

PS8553.O85Z85 2005 C843'.54 C2004-906957-8

Artist Ody Saban. « Lilith avance comme ça, parfois ». 1984 (31 x 22,5 cm. Aquarelle sur papier. jpg).

All rights reserved. Except for the quotation of short passages for the purposes of criticism and review, no part of this publication may be reproduced, stored in a retrieval system, or transmitted, in any form or by any means – electronic, mechanical, photocopying, recording, or otherwise – without the prior written permission of the publisher : Human Sciences Monograph Series, R. D. Parker Building, Laurentian University, Ramsey Lake Road, Sudbury, Ontario, Canada, P3E 2C6.

Human Sciences Mongraph Series 9
Série monographique en sciences humaines 9
Sudbury, Ontario, Canada
Copyright © Elizabeth Sabiston 2005

To my dear mother and father,
who gave me the gift of language

BY THE SAME AUTHOR

The Prison of Womanhood : Four Provincial Heroines in Nineteenth-Century Fiction. London : Macmillan, and New York : St. Martin's Press, 1987. ISBN : 0-333-41941-3 (Macmillan) ; 1-311-80-2 (St. Martin's)

Translation and Introduction: Hédi Bouraoui, *Return to Thyna.* Saratoga Springs, New York : Éditions Les Mains Secrètes, 2004. ISBN 0-9665360-4-5.

Contents

INTRODUCTION

By way of brief preface to this text, I should explain how I arrived at this particular thesis as a means of tying together the very dense, highly figurative, "exploding" novels of Hédi Bouraoui, which are loaded with neologisms, borrowings from other languages, linguistic experiments.

In the past I have written numerous articles and chapters of books on Hédi Bouraoui's poetry, as well as his academic books and essays. When he began to experiment with the novel form – first with *L'Icônaison: roman-poème* (1985) and *Rose des Sables: conte* (1997) – he became more and more concerned with narratology. Having the advantage of reading each novel as it appeared, I began to perceive the "Ariadne's thread" that would guide readers through the Bouraoui labyrinth. The heroine of *Rose des Sables* points the way from mythic elements drawn from the Thousand and One Nights and the oral folk tradition of the Maghreb to female protagonists who, while retaining symbolic dimensions, are nonetheless conceived with a dose of psychological realism: these are women with minds of their own and their own tales to tell.

While teaching *Retour à Thyna* (1995,1997) at York University to my undergraduate Women in Literature course, the enthusiasm of my students, many of them multicultural, encouraged my efforts to highlight the all-important female dimension of Bouraoui's texts. In particular, I have focused on the rebellion of his heroines against the traditional role of Muse

(Dante's Beatrice, Petrarch's Laura, Shakespeare's Dark Lady), and their appropriation of the supposedly "male" role of artist or writer.

As Bouraoui's boundless energy has been directed more and more towards strong narrative flow, with which he plays in a postmodernist vein, he also associates these narratives increasingly with the female voice, as historically the latter has been associated with the rise of the novel. This voice emerges with growing clarity and assertiveness as we move from Koï in *Bangkok Blues* (1994) to Héloïse, aptly named for the medieval scholar and rebel in love more than for Rousseau's heroine, in *La Composée* (2001), and, in a different way, to the first submissive, then resistant Lisa/Palimpseste in *La Femme d'entre les lignes* (2002). I felt that I was discovering the role of female narratology in Bouraoui's texts in the same measure as the author was discovering it. In fact, ironically, because of his first name, unfamiliar outside the Maghreb, and often taken for the female name "Heidi," Bouraoui is frequently mistaken for a female academic, a mistake reinforced by his emphasis on female aspirations.

The novelist-critic Reynolds Price argues chauvinistically that male writers provide "many successful entries into female consciousness... Tolstoy's Natasha and Anna, Flaubert's Emma, Hardy's Tess and Sue, Dreiser's Carrie and Joyce's Molly" (16), but that women writers – George Eliot, Willa Cather, Toni Morrison – cannot make the same gender leap because they are excluded from male psychosexual experience. Thus, for instance, none of George Eliot's heroes "is revealed in the core of his erotic nature" (18) – a questionable assumption at best, when one considers Lydgate in *Middlemarch*, whose sexuality traps him in a soul-destroying marriage.

Bouraoui's excursions into the female consciousness escape any presumption of male superiority, for his heroines are constantly surprising, rounding upon the men who would make them into passive muses or inspirations. They are intent on stepping "up from the pedestal," to echo the title of Aileen Kraditor's 1960's book, or, more vigorously, on "striking back"against conformity, passivity, subjugation. Much like Willa Cather's muse for a male narrator in *My Antonia* (1918), the heroine's strong point of view is suggested "*entre les lignes*," between the lines, by her dialogue, her actions, her own storytelling, letters and documents. As Cather warns us about the unreliability of her male narrator, Jim Burden, Bouraoui's male narrators and central cosnsciousnesses are interrogated, often belied, by their chosen muse. There is, moreover, a progression in this figure from the silent Koï in *Bangkok Blues* to the autonomous artist Héloïse in *La Composée* and the archetypal "woman between the lines," Lisa/Palimpseste, who emerges from between the lines of the male narrator's text with her own agenda and her own art. Lisa, in fact, debunks the narrator's text and his idealization of her by creating her own text and remaking him into the fictional figure of Virebaroud. Yes, Bouraoui's are heroines created by a male consciousness, but one which respects "the otherness of the other,"as he puts it, reflecting in art the attempts to create dialogue in life.

It is noteworthy that as far back as 1983, in *The Critical Strategy*, Bouraoui was using Simone de Beauvoir's attack against the traditional role of woman as muse to bolster his own theory of the critical dialectic. As Beauvoir wrote, "Man feminizes the ideal he sets up before him as the essential Other, because woman is the material representation of alterity... Woman is Soul and Idea, but she also is a mediatrix between them..." (Beauvoir 202; quoted by Bouraoui 9). As Bouraoui summarizes the conventional view, "She is muse or inspiration, but not herself a creator save in the biological sense" (9). If the critic mediates between text and reader, as woman is supposed to mediate between man and nature, Bouraoui stresses that the eroticism generated by the critical act does not imply a female critic and a male text, or the converse, but "the passion and power generated by the critical 'mediatrix' between work and reader " (10). The ideal, although unattainable, is one of fusion of the critical and creative acts.

To situate the first six novels – they won't be the last – in the broader spectrum of his career, Hédi Bouraoui coined the term "Transculturalism" and made it a dominant concept in the establishment of the Canadian identity. University Professor Emeritus of French Studies at York University, as scholar, cultural critic, poet and novelist, he has done, and continues to do, pioneering work in creating dialogue both within Canada, and between and among Canada and the United States, the Maghreb, Subsaharan Africa, France, the Caribbean, Italy, the Mediterranean basin (north and south), eastern Europe, and the Far East. In French Studies, for some time as its Chair, Hédi Bouraoui designed curriculum in Maghrebian and Franco-Ontarian literature, the first in Canada, as well as promoting Francophone studies in general. As Master of Stong College he initiated cross-cultural studies through the College Curriculum, and forged links to the Ontario and federal Ministries of Multiculturalism. The *Tales of Heritage I* and *II* publications, based on legends of the various ethnic groups composing the Canadian mosaic, including the First Nations, grew out of the Stong Transcultural identity. Consisting of imaginative recreations of the legends in the original language, and in French and English, by Professor Bouraoui, with illustrations by renowned Canadian artists Saul Field and Jean Townsend, the project was funded by a Wintario grant from the Ontario Ministry of Multiculturalism. Outside the University, Hédi Bouraoui was one of the founders of the African Literature Association (ALA), particularly of Maghreb Studies within it. He subsequently served as President of the ALA. Thus Hédi Bouraoui's projects as academic and creative writer reflect the same concerns with *Transculturalism*, but also with *Transpoïétique*, the breaking of genres and formal experimentation with poetry and poetic prose. The progression of his career from the 1960's to the present shows a varied body of work drawing upon diverse cultural dialogues, demonstrating that he fulfilled his early promise as a Fulbright Exchange Scholar in North America.

In October 2002 the Canada-Maghreb Centre opened at Stong, the result of a generous gift of books and documents and an endowment to York University from Hédi Bouraoui. The Centre houses a collection of Francophone literatures, principally from the Maghreb and Francophone Ontario, but also from Subsaharan Africa, the Caribbean, Québec, and the Maritimes. It is the first research center in the field in Canada, and one of only three in North America. Its role is to foster research in the two principal areas of the Maghreb – an important postcolonial discourse little understood in North America – and Francophone Ontario – which includes not only the "*écrivains de souche*," but also new Canadians writing in French.

Based in Toronto, Hédi Bouraoui was born in Sfax, Tunisia, educated in France and the United States, and has lived and taught for many years in Canada, where he appreciates and celebrates the Canadian mosaic, cultural diversity, and tolerance. As he has written, "La Culture est le chemin de la tolérance/Et l'ignorance ne peut être que source de violence" ("Poésie," *Vers et l'Envers*, 1982). He frequently draws parallels between his mother country, Tunisia, the "plaque tournante de l'Afrique méditerranéenne," and Canada, since both have been colonized at one time, and both are the products of successive waves of immigrants added to the founding populations, the Berbers in the Maghreb, the First Nations in Canada. A member of the Royal Society of Canada, and first Chevalier, then Officier des Palmes académiques, he has served in several administrative capacities at York University. He has organized several international conferences on

Creativity and Criticism, on Francophone literatures, on Maghrebian literature, on the Canadian Alternative.

Hédi Bouraoui is the author of a formidable body of both creative and scholarly works. Although rooted in Toronto, he is a latter-day Ulysses traveling throughout the world, "Wandering Forever." His twenty volumes of poetry, like his novels, reflect this eternal pilgrimage: space exploration (*Éclate Module*, 1972); transcending boundaries, geographical and linguistic (*Sans Frontières/Without Boundaries*, in French and English); the Caribbean (*Haïtuvois, suivi de Antillades*, 1980); Macedonia (*Struga, suivi de Margelle d'un festival*, 2003); and in another vein, *Illuminations autistes* (2003), filling the gap of silence for autistic children.

He is the author of a poetic drama, *Immensément Croisés*, short stories, a tale, *Rose des Sables*, which won the Prix du Salon du Livre de Toronto in 1998, one novel-poem, *L'Icônaison*, and six novels to date: *Bangkok Blues* (1994); *Retour à Thyna* (1995, new edition 1997), which has been awarded the Grand Prix littéraire de la Ville de Sfax (1995) and the Prix spécial du jury des Plumes d'or Comar (1997); *La Pharaone* (1998), which was also awarded the Grand Prix du jury des Plumes d'or Comar (1998); *Ainsi parle la Tour CN* (1999), nominated for the Ontario Trillium Award, and awarded the Prix du Salon du Livre de Toronto (2000); *La Composée* (2001), and *La Femme d'entre les lignes* (2002). He has also been awarded the Prix France-Maghreb de L'ADELF.

As an academic, he has from the beginning been interested in experiments with genre, as in his first book of criticism, *Structure intentionnelle du "Grand Meaulnes": vers le poème romancé* (1976), which views the 1913 novel of Alain-Fournier as a "poème romancé." In *The Critical Strategy* (1983) he developed his own critical theory by analyzing other postmodern schools, but transcending them through his notion of creative criticism, again breaking boundaries between the creative and critical acts. His current criticism applies this experimental critical theory to Francophone literatures around the world, particularly from the Maghreb, but also Franco-Ontario, the Caribbean, and Subsaharan Africa. Among his other critical and scholarly works are: *Créaculture I* and *Créaculture II* (1971), on French culture and civilization set against a North American background; *La Francophonie à l'estomac* (1995), developing and applying critical theory to francophone literature, as well as countless articles in learned journals. He has edited a number of texts, notably *La Littérature franco-ontarienne: État des lieux* (2000). As both creator and critic, his major concern has been with transculturalism (his term), the building of bridges between cultures, as well as between people, and notably between male and female, gender and genre.[1]

As I have said elsewhere:

> Bouraoui is a one-man example of Transculturalism in that he has lived and worked on three continents [Africa, Europe, and North America]. [...] He has said in an interview with Édouard Maunick that his patrie is "la Patrie de l'Homme," that he is "un homme de partout." [...] His desire to make connections between and among his native and adopted cultures, and the cultures he has visited, has also driven him to break traditional boundaries of language and poetry. (Sabiston in *Échosmos* 14)

Thus he has attempted to build bridges between literary genres as well as between people, breaking down barriers between and among drama, fiction, and poetry. "Drame poétique" and "roman-poème" are frequent generic rubrics which subvert the reader's traditional responses.

My own approach to his creative work could be best described as phenomenological, under the influence of the critics of consciousness, Georges Poulet, Paul De Man, *et al.* I have been especially privileged as a phenomenologist to witness the creative process as each novel appears (and even to have read them in manuscript). As a feminist critic, as well as a phenomenologist, I am sensitive to the plurality of criticisms, and tolerant of any which illuminate the work. As Bouraoui emphasizes in *The Critical Strategy*, each work dictates its own critical methodology: "... I have allowed each text to generate its own critical method, to reveal its own code, without imposing a grid on it, whether it be semiotics, hermeneutics, psychoanalysis, Marxism, etc." (7). I have undergone some of the same influences as Bouraoui, who was attracted to the phenomenology of Poulet and De Man "because of its emphasis on, empathy with, and attempted re-creation of, an author's original creative process " (115). Bouraoui paraphrases De Man's stress, in *Blindness and Insight* (1971) on critical empathy, or fusion with the work: "... the critic's greatest insights occur at moments of blindness to theory; yet the theory is a necessary precondition to these privileged moments " (131). I give due recognition to Bouraoui's stress on a criticism generated by each individual work, and to the creative-critical process. As Geoffrey Hartman said, "I am text-bound." The other theory relevant to Bouraoui, and dating farther back, is Sartrean existentialism: Bouraoui's

---

[1] Bouraoui defines transculturalism in his texts, *Créaculture I* and *II* (throughout) and *The Canadian Alternative* 104-10.

work shows a profound *engagement*, a humanistic commitment, to openness, tolerance between genders, genres, cultures, young and old. As we have seen, his re-visioning of the muse owes a debt to Beauvoir's groundbreaking existential critique of socially programmed gender definitions.

In 1999 Bouraoui was awarded the Prix du Nouvel-Ontario for "his contributions in the field of poetry, fiction and interculturalism." The prize is given to an artist who has had a significant impact on francophone Ontario, and Bouraoui is called a "voyageur inlassable à travers le monde, engagé sereinement dans tous les domaines de la Francophonie" (*Communiqué de "La Nuit sur l'Étang"*, Université Laurentienne, 6 mars 1999).

Although Bouraoui considers *L'Icônaison* (1985) to be his first step towards a novel, marking the transition from poetry to fiction, I have chosen to begin with the second novel, *Bangkok Blues.* While *L'Icônaison* is a *poème romancé à la Alain-Fournier*, and therefore somewhat problematic as a narrative, in *Bangkok Blues* we have the fully developed characterization I consider to be the hallmark of the novel. Moreover, in Koï we have for the first time (outside of his poetry) Bouraoui's radical re-visioning of the traditional Muse figure. In addition, we are transported to Thailand, a country that is completely strange to both author and reader. Bouraoui creates a Francophone novel about a country whose culture and language he studies intently and empathetically. The novel thus becomes a testing ground for his theory of Transculturalism. *Bangkok Blues* leaps to the Far East from the Occident, and to a Thai woman who inspires a male protagonist. We will join them on that journey.

Hédi Bouraoui

Bangkok blues

Roman

Vermillon

I

Bangkok Blues :

Bouraoui's « Correspondances », or, « Les parfums, les couleurs et les sons se répondent »

Baudelaire and Dante

Hédi Bouraoui's *Bangkok Blues* (1994) bridges the gap between lyric poetry and poetic novel, a step already anticipated in the earlier *L'Icônaison*, which is more poetry than novel, but tends towards the latter. *Bangkok Blues* is composed of incantatory prose epiphanies, which make it at least in part a prose poem. Its subjects include language, past and present, the gap between rich and poor and between cultures. Bouraoui's title, *Bangkok Blues*, suggests at least one of his possible inspirations: Baudelaire's *Fleurs du Mal*, in particular the famous « Correspondances. » The blues is both a musical form derived from the African American tradition of dealing with pain, and a color suggestive of sea and sky. As Baudelaire wrote in « Correspondances », « Les parfums, les couleurs et les sons se répondent. » In *Bangkok Blues* Bouraoui invokes all the senses – sound, sight, smell, touch – to re-create the world of the unknown, curiously cosmopolitan Bangkok, Thailand.

The other master more obviously invoked is Dante: Bangkok is at times seen as the infernal city. The epigraph is from Dante: "Love which moves the sun and other stars" [L'amor che move il sole e l'altre stelle], and the novel is divided into fourteeen cantos, derived from music. The novel also traces a quest for origins, and one of its paradigms is the Biblical book of Genesis, as well as a Jungian collective unconscious. But the origins it seeks are those of language. The hero/sometime narrator's name is Virgulius, derived from the Roman poet Virgil, whom Dante evoked as his guide in the underworld. It is Virgil who wrote the epic poem about the founding of Rome, the *Aeneid*, and who describes man as a tree, rooted deeply in the earth but reaching upwards to the heavens. At one point, the questor Virgulius remarks that he personifies the tree of languages: « Je deviens l'arbre d'abondance, aux branches perlées de citrons dans lesquels on a mis des pièces d'or, des pierres de jade » (114). French, English, and Thai are all utilized, as well as Arabic, English-French, English-Thai. There are references to sub-Saharan African and Caribbean folk legends and myths, specifically Haitian, as well as language in general: « ... accompagné d'Erzuli, déesse de l'amour et de la beauté. À nos côtes Damballah-Ouédo, dieu des sources et des rivières. » And Haiti and Africa are fused: « À travers la magie d'Haïti, mon Afrique était ici entière dans la souffrance et dans la joie émaillant mon intermonde » (115).

Onomastics: What's in a Name?

Virgulius's Latin origins are referred to directly at one point: « Virgulius participe à l'aventure mot à mot. Parfois il perd son latin... » (99). It is evident that he is North African, a region conquered in ancient times by the Romans, one among a whole series of invaders, of whom the last were the French, leaving their mark on the indigenous population both genetically and linguistically. If Virgulius is a modern Virgil, however, it is Koï, the young Thai woman, who is the guide and mentor. She is compared to Dante's Beatrice, the guide through the Paradiso, but if Bangkok is an ambiguous Inferno/Earthly Paradise, she is also the guide through the Underworld, Virgil. Virgulius's rival for Koï is her dead father, and here the comparison to Petrarch's Laura comes in: « L'un embrasse Laure comme un Pétrarque octogénaire balbutiant ses Canzoni... », while « L'autre reçoit d'en haut sa Béatrice. Elle fond sur lui dans une Divine Comédie... » (35). Virgulius, one assumes, like Dante, is "midway the journey of this life" (thirty-five for Dante), and the experience of Bangkok and of Koï, who herself embodies Bangkok, « la femme-cité, » marks the turning point in his life.

Koï's name in Thai means « le petit doigt », or little finger, the fifth born in a family of ten, and the imagery of fingers and hands which pervades the text reinforces the notion that she is the mentor or guide. She is always referred to as "Koï thaï."

Virgulius's name has another source, as well as that of the Roman poet. It is a play upon « virgule », or the comma, which marks a pause in the sentence, as a period of contemplation in Virgulius's life: « Quand on aime, il faut fuir pour ne pas mourir. Vivre cet amour comme une virgule, le temps unique d'une pause sans poser de limite aux cœurs qui s'enlacent » (144). The word play suggests that Virgulius *pauses* over his love, without im*posing* a limit on it. Towards the end he describes the significance of his idealized love for Koï, who is in fact poetry, or a muse, like Beatrice and Laura, rather than a realistically conceived woman.

Shifting Narrative Voices

In the last three cantos, there is a shift in narrative voice. All three are titled, unlike the first eleven. Canto XII is entitled « Carnet du Pinceau Volant, » suggesting that Bouraoui is using a technique he described so well in his study of Alain-Fournier's *Le Grand Meaulnes*, that is, the incorporation of a notebook or journal within the text. But the « Pinceau volant » is a free-ranging artist's brush, emphasizing that Bouraoui is borrowing from all the arts, in a form of Baudelairean synesthesia, to transcend the verbal. Is it Virgulius transcending his own limits? Thus, Koï's silence is eloquent, contrasted to the meaningless garrulity of her sister Joy. The names rhyme, and the sisters are alter egos. Koï, « la polytechnicienne du simple, » expresses herself splendidly in sensual smiles and nods. Thus, synesthesia, or « correspondances », fill the gaps of verbal communication. A brief reference to « échos proustiens » to describe the allure of the Thai language – in this case selling flesh – reminds us of the unity of senses in Proust's image of the madeleine, which triggers memory.

Canto XIII also draws our attention to the central theme of communication, « Journal du Bambou », and the last, Canto XIV, « Transe des Doigts: Mahori du fleuve à cinq variations », draws in not only the dominant finger/hand image, but specifically alludes to fingers playing on stringed instruments, a "Mahori" being a Thai string orchestra.

Virgulius's Quest: The Origins of Language

The artist figure in the text appears to be Virgulius, though the narrator of Canto XII, « le Pinceau volant », apparently distances himself from Virgulius's ambiguities and ambivalences: « Je ne prends pas le pouvoir de la bouche énigmatique de Virgulius » (135). Like Virgil's Aeneas, Virgulius crosses the sea to a new, strange land, not to found a city, but to *find* a city, and to express it in a new language based on the elements – earth, air, water, and fire – and on correspondences. The dominant religion, Buddhism, embraces the earth and the heavens. Thus, the Buddha statue viewed by Virgilius has one foot in the air, representing the circle of life, « la perspective cyclique », « l'esprit » and « la lettre », « la droite et la courbe » (27). Virgulius is perplexed at the start about how to write of Thailand in French, « avec mes mots d'Occident » (20). He views Bangkok as a « coquille vide », a city of ruins which has haunted his dreams. He wants to penetrate an unknown which lies beyond human language, to « transmettre ce qui résiste aux mots » (20). What he sees is a country of extremes, of ancient and modern, of poverty and wealth, juxtaposing traditional Asian temples, pagodas, palaces, and abject poverty, with « arrogant » twentieth-century skyscrapers (22).

The very first line of the novel signals a return to origins: « Ce voyage remonte le temps... » (9). We realize that the quest hero has ties to "my prosperous America" as well as to "the deserts of my Africa." He has flown from Roissy (Charles De Gaulle), so we know he is now living in France. Even in the plane he senses the « correspondances » of this complex city where, paraphrasing Baudelaire, « les couleurs et les sons font plus que se répondre; ils infusent tout mon être placé comme par miracle dans ce carrefour de civilisations, où l'Asiatique refuse de céder le pas au Gaulois ! » (21). Multicultural himself, but Occidental, he is nonetheless brought face to face with a country that is totally enigmatic, mysterious to him, with its extremes of poverty and wealth, of flesh and spirit, « nouveau pays de cocaïne et de chair après l'abandon honteux des colonies » (10). This statement is as cryptic as the country itself, as it was never literally colonized by the imperialist West. The term « postcolonial », in such wide use today, cannot be literally applied to Thailand: « Et Thaï, terre de liberté, n'a jamais été colonisé » (46). The correct term hasn't been invented for Thailand, since "Third World" has been labeled politically incorrect. It is a land of liberty which sometimes crosses the frontier into licence, even licentiousness.

Yet it is also a land subject to another hidden form of colonization – by tourists who think they can capture the essence of a culture on film: « Le temple devient le souk des clichés à emporter sur pellicules » (31). Virgulius links their invasion of Thailand with that of his native North Africa by slipping in the Arabic word for marketplace, « souk ». Photography – the ultimate realism – is linked with violence, as we see a Korean « mitrailler le paysage, de son appareil photo » (96). And everywhere the English language (especially American) imposes itself as the « seule lingua franca ». Moreover, « Ici, tant de touristes français de troisième ordre se comportent en Américains, sillonnent les lieux de pensées avilies » (11). Bouraoui adds an epic/Whitmanian catalogue of languages constituting this « Tour de Babel » (82). This is supplemented by equally Virgilian/Whitmanian lists, such as the string of sentences beginning with « Que »:

> Que d'années passées...
> Que d'algues moroses...
> Que de naïveté cultivée...
> Que de remous écartés... (36)

And a few pages later we find Virgulius's self-examination, repeating « suis-je », and echoing Montaigne's « Qui suis-je? » as well as, obviously, Dante's *Divine Comedy*:

> Suis-je au paradis perdu d'un amour qui veut être entendu?
> Suis-je dans l'enfer où l'espoir piège les corps torturés?
> Suis-je dans le purgatoire de l'attente qui veut bien
> croire à la renaissance d'un nouveau siècle? (44)

Love becomes a text for Virgulius, but he prefers a triumph of the imagination to reading an already-in-print book on Thailand: « Je ne l'ouvrirai jamais. Je préfère vivre dans la foule et dans le corps de la femme orchidée » (101). So the woman, Koï, becomes the book.

Metaphors of turned pages fill the text. When her father died four months ago, Virgulius's comment is « Tournée, la page du sacrifice » (49). And a little later, Virgulius says, « Que la page soit tournée dans le sable de nos déserts terrestres et lunaires », linking Eastern deserts (including Desert Storm and all the succeeding desert wars) and lunar landscapes (56).

Virgulius finds that the Orient liberates both him and his language from shame.

Koï, la Femme-Cité

If Koï is literature – « Koï, ma belle étrangère, ma littérature qui bouge » – the French woman, Françoise, tries to bring Virgulius back to his quasi-French heritage. Bouraoui uses yet another form of narrative, the epistolary, of Western origin, to convey Françoise's rebukes: « Mais tu rêves et tu as tout inventé, ce pays, trésor de chair au crépuscule de ta destinée » (40). A modern, less subtle version of Laclos' scheming Madame de Merteuil in *Les Liaisons dangereuses* (1782), she tries to make Koï into a woman like herself: « Une femme habituée aux brasseries parisiennes à la mode et au parfum reconnu ». But, remarks Virgulius, « ce genre de vie est déjà révolu ».

For Virgulius, Koï is the ideal « femme-cité », the spirit of the old Bangkok, not the modern « femme-cité à la chevelure folle » (23). Modern Bangkok is « cette terre tierce ... [qui] marie le défaut du manque et l'exaltation du surcroît » (10). Its center resembles a mango resisting opening, while the rest of the city seems swallowed up by water – canals, streams, rivers, the sea: « Un tout mouvant, sans limites » (11). It teems with a population of six million, more than 10% of the total Thai population, with « un air si pollué qu'il étoufferait les bœufs les plus robustes » (12). The inhabitants are so fatalistic that even the beggars fail to beg. The meat is fly-covered in the open-air market, and everything, especially female flesh, is for sale, like the meat. As Virgulius's driver says, « Avec de l'argent on peut tout acheter, le plaisir, la chair, le sanuk, tout » (13). Virgulius, of African, European, American heritage, intrigued by the unknown, « cette Asie extrême-orientale » (14), defines thus the purpose of his art, to create an « inter-essai », « non pour excaver de l'intérieur une ... confession du genre nouveau roman, mais pour saisir l'étrangeté inconnue... ». He is impelled by « ce désir virulent et vertigineux de quitter notre peau ». As a Bulgarian has described the artistic impulse, it is « une blessure qui propulse vers un ailleurs toujours repoussé, inassouvi, inaccessible » (14).

The lure of the unattainable is embodied in Koï, this startled « gazelle » he has perceived in the midst of « cette cité infernale de la surenchère charnelle » (16). She guides Virgulius through hell, and, like Beatrice, towards a lost paradise. Virgulius realizes that she seems to arise from his unconscious. She is a dream, a thought, « silence de lune qui émerveille les étoiles » (16), not coincidentally paraphrasing the epigraph from Dante.

The masseuses of the omnipresent massage parlors, or sex markets, skillfully manipulate their clients, in a perverse twist on Pascal, into a « vision ardente que la raison ne connaît pas ». Pascal, of course, was speaking of the heart, and love of God : « Le cœur a ses raisons que la raison ne connaît pas ». But here we are looking at lust, not love, whether human or divine. Thus Bangkok is a « femme-cité » in more ways than one, for it is a city which offers its women to the highest (or even the lowest) bidder.

Koï is identified more with the spirit of the older capital, Ayutthayâ, built in 1350 and razed by the Burmese in 1769. It was surrounded by three rivers for defense, and resembled an elephant's hoof. The white elephant is a totemic figure that appears throughout the text, something that is a "hard sell" in English, but valuable and rare in Thailand. The ruins of Ayutthayâ are a « musée de l'imaginaire des jours de gloire et de faste ».

Koï has protected herself with a vow of chastity, resisting sexual enslavement. Virgulius is also a « célibataire qui refuse de jouer le jeu de la chair à n'importe quel prix » (23). He is not Prince Charming, but « le roturier émigré, passant comme un ouragan dans ce pays ... de cocaïne et de chair » (35). Koï is a modest heroine who combines Oriental fatalism with the serene smile of, not the Mona Lisa, but the Buddha. And the Thai Buddha is all too human: he is one who has « goûté la chair » (155). The Buddhists are in quest of Nirvana, not the Holy Grail. But Virgulius points out the essential unity of all religions, « nécessaire[s] à notre survie sur cette terre de damnés »: « ... nous sommes nés sous le nouvel arc-en-ciel des fois qui barattent dans nos veines, sans jamais hurler leur croix christique, leur étoile de David, leur croissant lunaire ou leur roue bouddhique » (20).

The finger/hand image suggests Koï's creative role, evoking the fingers of the writer or musician or painter. Thus we have a marriage of the arts. Koï breaks the Oriental stereotype; she is not submissive, but helps Virgulius cross frontiers (38). Her innocence is like a bird hidden beneath one's shirt. She is an « être de silence », « mon autobiographie plurielle », says Virgulius. He also refers to « nos corps textes », and calls her a collaborator: « Nous sommes deux d'avoir ouvert ton livre complice, Koï. Ce livre de délices qui reçoit la vie comme une lettre, sans l'ouvrir » (39). But she also creates him.

Virgulius associates her with the North African khamsa, a symbol in the form of a stylized hand pointing downward, intended to bring good fortune to the wearer. The khamsa unifies the novel. If Virgulius is the migrating writer, the « forgeron des mots », Koï is « le petit doigt » who will always accompany him: « ... je serai toujours avec toi » (25). She is in a sense the ideal reader, or audience. He addresses her from the start as « tu », breaking with tradition to create intimacy. The hand carrying her seal becomes a « pendentif khamsa qui nous protège dans les coulisses de la haine et des mésententes » (60).

If the khamsa is a kind of hieroglyphic to be decoded, the Thai language itself is composed of ideograms, to be deciphered by the stranger Virgulius, a language that again brings to mind Baudelaire's « forêt de symboles » : « La nature est un temple où de vivants piliers... ».

Comparative Religions

Koï is also an Eve in the garden of Eden, and Bangkok itself is the serpent of temptation, cut up by rivers « comme un serpent coupé en rondelles » (26). Joy recounts a folk tale about the serpent: if a woman encounters it, she will meet her man. If it stings, the marriage will be soon. If it is killed by a relative, it means that she will be protected from a marriage that would not be good for her (55). The Thais themselves have been expelled from their original Eden, the capital Ayutthayâ, moving to the south to escape their enemies: « Les Thaïs ne peuvent aller plus loin » (27). The Buddhist cosmogony, traïbumi phra ruang, is, like the modern Bangkok, a « monde d'amour et de souffrance, de jouissance et de douleur, du paradis et de l'enfer, de Brahma et de son esprit désincarné » (28). It is the "Siamese twin" of Virgulius, Pierre, who succumbs to the lure of Bangkok flesh, "Siamese twin" suggesting both that he accompanies Virgulius, and that he is an alter ego or doppelgänger, much as Joy is for her sister. It is Pierre who seeks to « se gorger du sexe à gogo dans ce pays réputé pour ses orgies inimaginables » (53). His name, « Pierre », or stone, links him with the « coquille vide » of corrupt modern-day Bangkok. Through the guide Koï, Virgulius finds Dante's « paradis perdu » after traversing the inferno and purgatory. It is through Koï that Virgulius « remonte le cours de mes origines » (37).

The word "main" is repeated several times in Canto VI, like a voice without vocalization, orange blossoms flying in the wind, or tasting a virginal spirit: « ... je savoure encore de Koï thaï la main... » (54). Koï becomes "Koï-livre, »with virginal pages (59). Thanks to her, Virgulius is neither alienated nor fragmented. He is inscribed in the tradition of poets of the city: from Virgil's Aeneid to Baudelaire's *Spleen de Paris*, to Whitman's New York, T.S. Eliot's "Unreal City" (London), Sandburg's Chicago, Nikki Giovanni's Newark. Virgil's Rome, Baudelaire's Paris, Eliot's London are simultaneously real cities and poetic constructs; but, with the exception of Giovanni's Newark, these are masculine constructs, whereas Koï, in an important sense, creates herself in a purely female way, transcending the limits of the real, as opposed to the written, Bangkok. She is a lotus closed in on itself, after her frustrated marriage to Chowarit (93), but she also reminds Virgulius of his native olive tree. Looking at the tomb of Queen Suriyothai, who lost her life saving her husband's, as Koï saves Virgulius from futility and ambiguity, he finds himself in « cet éden perdu » (61).

Koï resists all national boundaries, just as she would have fascism or Hitler (109). If Voltaire's Candide retreats from the reality of war, torture, man's inhumanity, to « cultiver son jardin », Virgulius cultivates his « jardin intérieur » which is, in the final analysis, unlike Candide's, edenic, rather than escapist (39). Buddhism is implicitly compared to the other great religions of the world, with references to the Maghrebian/Islamic tradition conveyed by the voice of the griot, or official talespinner (57). A Bangkok tower resembles a minaret, complete with a muezzin calling worshippers to prayer (60). Virgulius refers to a black Buddha, moving the image to sub-Saharan Africa. A pagoda resembles the Tower of Pisa (61). Christianity is evoked when we are told to render unto Buddha that which belongs to Buddha (as to Caesar) (119), and in the phrase, « Que de chemins de Damas et de chemins de croix! » (93). The Marabout suggests the influence of Haiti and voodoo, and Bouraoui/Virgulius draws upon Arabic and Sanskrit to communicate (115). He finds « le sourire de nirvana dans le mektoub de Koï », fusing Buddhist and Islamic notions of paradise and fate. A global bonding manifests itself. Virgulius argues with himself, using the framework of the Thousand and One Nights (whose putative author is a woman, Scheherazade, the archetypal female artist) whether the poet is a liar, or speaks a higher poetic truth (86).

The first eleven cantos seem to lead to a form of birth in Eden. The little blonde girl Achara, whose Thai name in Arabic means "sign", adopts Virgulius and Koï as surrogate parents: « Elle nous a choisis, couple avant la lettre du baiser » (125). Not literally parents, perhaps not literally even a couple, she chooses them as spiritual and symbolic generators of her own sign language. She too is a budding artist, sketching « fraternité » and

« égalité » (126). « Égalité » depicts female twins (not the male Siamese twins Virgulius and Pierre). On the next page we read that Koï is also twinned, close and distant like a queen of life and death in Virgulius's garden. Koï recounts the folk legend told her by her mother Kannika: « Dans nos traditions, quand la personne vient de l'enfer la mère crie, quand elle vient du ciel, la mère rit, quand elle vient de la terre, la mère oublie." Virgulius comments, « Mektoub avant l'écrit », again wedding two folk traditions, but also contrasting fate (Mektoub) to « l'écrit », the exercise of free will (128).

The birth is that of language, or perhaps communion, going « au-delà des mots » (129). Their quest is towards riches that transcend words, linking many myths and languages that call on universal values (130). Virgulius describes Koï as « la modeste paume de ma main libérée, complice de sa caresse » (131). He himself is a seismograph (like Fitzgerald's Great Gatsby), reflecting local quakes and turbulence, both natural and man-made..

Virgulius's narration actually ends with a bitter, cynical letter from Françoise, addressing him as « Mon cher Virzombi », "Vir" being "man" in Latin, but a zombie, in Haiti, is one of the living dead. She mocks the North African language: « J'aime beaucoup ces vents chauds, sirocco et harmattan (quels noms bizarres!) » (132). But her own command of languages is mocked by Virgulius: "You are eu peine in ze asse, dit-elle en son anglais de Queen qui reste lamentablement français » (91). She also refers to his calling her « la rose de sable qui frappe les esprits » (133). But the last word is his, an affirmation of his experience with Koï:

> ... ma nuit de mots est plus belle que le jour... Si je n'avais pas fait ce voyage intérieur avec Koï thaï, j'aurais perdu le contact avec mon être le plus profond. Je serais passé à côté de la vie. Mais non. Je suis dynamité du dedans. Cet accent de vérité virgulise le silence de Koï qui semble me dire, *à chaque amour nouveau, l'on regagne son innocence.* (134)

The quotation is extremely rich and dense. Lyricism is the product of night – of dreams, some erotic, some not, of an oneiric state – rather than broad daylight and reality. Virgulius's important travels take place within his own soul, with Koï thaï as the enabler. He is vibrating like a seismograph, dynamited from within in an act of destruction which is also creative. From it a higher poetic truth emerges, from the fusion of Virgulius's pauses, reflections, and Koï's silences. But the passage ends on a cryptic, even problematic note: granted that Koï is the "new love", other than perhaps the waspish Françoise, we have no indication of any serious previous love. And we have just been told that Koï is an ideal, something special (whose own prior love was a failure). There seems, therefore, to be no question of another love, except on the imaginative, poetic level – unless Virgulius feels that every experience with Koï is a new beginning.

In Canto XII the « Pinceau volant » takes over the narration, describing a variant on the Last Supper, the « Banquet final » in « un restaurant cosmogonique », serving « la nourriture terrestre » (echo of Gide). The hand images take on a new level of meaning with the incense sticks which « ressemblent aux doigts emplâtrés de henne ». The thumb represents joy, also the name of Koï's sister; the index celebrates glory and power. The middle finger plays on its ambiguity. It is capped in green, which represents longevity to the Chinese, diabolism to the French, and is a sacred color to Moslems. The narrator comments that all are clearly defined, except the little finger, « citadelle de runes qui fait chatoyer le vent, la pluie, le ciel, les étoiles » – yet another echo of the epigraph from Dante. He continues, when an incense stick burns down, a work of art disappears forever, suggesting the ephemeral nature of art, the « pause » or « virgule » (137) – and perhaps the reclaimed innocence of the passage cited above, when the artist begins a new creation..

The « Pinceau volant » sees himself as the bodyguard « de ce couple de l'impossible » (138). Even the beds in their hotel room are textual rather than sexual: they are "twin" beds, the recurrent motif of twinning. The question is raised, is the relationship not consummated, or consummated like the incense sticks – that is, burned up, like a completed work of art? The beds « ont l'air de deux pages blanches géantes », suggesting that consummation is a false problematic, raised literally by Pierre Karch, who thinks that Françoise's « lettre de rupture, envoyée d'Afrique, précipite la « nuit blanche » (141) de Vir (l'homme) et de Koï (coït?) ... » Rather, the beds are an open book, foreshadowed by the « femme-livre » [libre?] whose symbols need to be read, « ce qui va réorienter l'ontologique du côté du transpoétique » (138). The « inter-dit » is both "the forbidden", and what passes between the lines, or Virgulius's « inter-essai ».

In this Canto it becomes clear that Koï's role as Eve figure is emphasized: « Ève jardin, c'est Djezia qui psalmodie le cantique des cantiques » (139). Djezia is the heroine of *La Geste hilalienne*, translated and interpreted by Lucienne Saâda. *La Geste hilalienne* is the Odyssey or Aeneid of North

Africa. Moreover, Djezia is reciting the « cantique des cantiques », or the Song of Solomon from the Biblical Old Testament, which uses human sexuality as a metaphor for the love of God – in this case, for the dedication to creativity. The frame of reference is both Moslem and Judeo-Christian. The Song of Solomon gestures in the direction of inter-racial love relationships: the mistress is "black, but comely." Moreover, Koï is not only twinned with Joy, but with Virgulius himself as a soulmate. The lover in Song of Solomon is running about the streets, as Virgulius does in Bangkok, in quest of the ideal union of flesh and spirit. Both lovers are as obsessively single-minded as Virgulius and Koï. Their relationship draws on all the senses, producing the « calme et volupté » of « Correspondances »: « Le toucher, la vue, l'ouïe, l'odorat, le goût se répondent » (141).

If Virgulius gives birth to poetry, Koï is an Eve who actually creates Virgulius, but on the spiritual level, not the biological: « Koï vient de créer en face de nous, et *in vitro*, un Virgulius sorti de ses entrailles silencieuses... Ton silence, Koï, a donné naissance à ce Vir, pierre angulaire de son dire » (143). Koï is a Magna Mater, or Earth Mother, the "Mother of us all." Her silence creates Virgulius's words. If "Vir" (man) rhymes with « dire » (speech) in French, it is implied that not only Virgulius, but Koï is the "Word Made Flesh." Christ built his Church on the stone (« pierre »), which in this passage refers not only to the Siamese twin of Virgulius, but also to the Church. The « *pierre angulaire* » also refers to the sharp (phallic?) letter "V" itself.

Canto XIII, « Journal du Bambou, » continues to evoke his Eden, « ce paysage de rêve », of the Book of Genesis: « Nous sommes là dans le chaos de la jouissance, le big bang de tous les créateurs » (147).

In Canto XIV, orchestrated by the Mahori, the « convoyeur de bateaux » lifts his thumb (150), and « On nous montre du doigt ». Love itself becomes art, once expressed: « Une fois dit, notre amour ne nous appartient plus, comme le livre jeté bouteille à la mer se délivre de l'emprise de son auteur. It is as if the book itself were a newborn baby, "de-livered," or "de-booked," and thereby freed from its author's conscious intention. To « dé-livre" is to free oneself, as well as to deliver the book. If the bottle thrown into the sea with its message reminds us of Edgar Allan Poe, the book set free from its author recalls Chaucer's releasing his work from his control: "Go, little book!" The narrator refers to « ce livre de ma khamsa, » a complex symbol for Bouraoui. Not only a mythic protector from the evil eye, this schematized hand also suggests brother/sisterhood, freedom from materialism, and above all creativity. Bouraoui's 1986 poem, « Khamsa Triomphante, » provides a gloss on the role of Koï:

> Triomphante la Khamsa, cette main mauresque déroute
> Le sort, conjure l'œil mauvais du tort. L'Œil et la Nuit
> Font écouler la somnolence des voix pour investir le bec du politique.
> ...
> Et la démarche circulaire et la pensée en colimaçon
> Et l'imaginaire qui tourne en rond...
> Ma main, ma source.
> ...
> Alors tu planteras dans tes sillons les haillons de ta pensée originelle
> Ton sol imbibera l'encre de ta sagesse et les œillets
> De la tendresse orneront les fronts des gouverneurs-épouvantails.

« Entre pouce et index », Koï says, « Je n'oublierai jamais your excellent teach of touch" (151). Their bodies are described as « les corps alphabets. »

This Canto fuses birth and death, and dwells in paradox: « L'enfant est les parents couple, car la mémoire empèche la maternité ». The « revolutionary diva" proclaims, « Nul ne peut concevoir sans avoir goûté la mort » (153). The theme is identified elsewhere by Bouraoui as « amourir. »[1] Virgulius writes of having conjured up in the unconscious « l'obscur désir de naître et de mourir » (156).

The hand/khamsa image climaxes in this last Canto. Koï says to Virgulius, « Je suis toujours avec toi. Je suis ton petit doigt. I don't fly to Paris. » She is both presence and absence. The narrator describes her function and influence: « ... ce petit doigt, seul scribe à pénétrer dans l'oreille pour lui insuffler la parole auriculaire qui ne mutile pas de son amour. Lui ne revendique aucun droit puisqu'ils sont tous deux à posséder le petit doigt et la virgule » (154).

Koï is all women in one: wife, lover, sister, mother, aunt, grandmother (156). Perhaps this is too much weight, however, for one character to bear. If the novel has a fault, it resides with Koï thaï, who seems to be more symbol than reality, whereas we come to know Virgulius, with all his human failings, and even the foil Françoise, whom we grasp through her mean-spirited epistolary style. There is a problem with a character whose creativity is expressed only through silence which inspires a lover/narrator who, presumably, writes the book. Her function seems to bring her dangerously

---

[1] *La Pharaone* (Tunis: L'Or du Temps, 1998).

close to the Muse that was Beatrice or Laura. Nonetheless, she anticipates Bouraoui's later heroines, culminating in Francine/Hatshepsut of *La Pharaone* and Héloïse of *La Composée*, both of whom embody the recurrent theme, "The Muse Strikes Back." She is a beginning, a necessary first step in the evolution of Bouraoui's heroines. Nathaniel Hawthorne once said of his « romances » (novels, we would say) that they have one foot in Cloud Cuckooland, one in reality. Koï thaï often seems to exist more in fantasy than in psychological realism, unlike the other characters. Her role in the text seems most appropriate to a poetic fabliau.

The novel ends with a unity of the elements, as of the aspects of woman: the lovers are baptized in the sea, the incense earlier represented fire, the novel is of the earth, and at the end the adventurer-hero takes off into the air: « Le pouce et l'index s'arrondissent, se frôlent, s'embrassent, zéro heure! Les trois autres doigts prennent de l'aile, l'avion décolle » (157).[2]

The female, haloed with imagery of the protective, inspiring hand or khamsa, is therefore seen as a ministering angel, the unifying force. She accomplishes a fusion of the elements, of male and female, of cultures erasing national boundaries, of the five senses, as she herself is all women in one. Twinning many of the characters reinforces the theme of fusion.

Koï participates by silence and gestures; perhaps "Koï thaï"suggests a kind of aesthetic "coitus interruptus." Although Virgulius creates with words, he is most successful with the pause conveyed by one source of his name, « virgule. » Better than any word of love he utters or writes is the tender gesture of settling his jacket around her shoulders. The cross-fertilization of word and silence is reminiscent of the Symbolist poets, who all trace their origin back to Baudelaire.

Virgulius succeeds in communicating only when the « Pinceau volant » takes over, whose instrument is paint, not words. Moreover, he is a brush « volant » who is able to take flight, to soar, through visual elements. The

---

[2] Robert Elbaz notes that Bouraoui undermines the apparent circularity of the narrative, and the reader's expectations of a resolution: « À un premier niveau, il semblerait que la structure est circulaire, puisque le récit commence avec un atterrissage et finit avec un décollage; le narrateur aurait ainsi accompli sa mission et découvert sa vérité. Or nous savons par ailleurs, étant donné le travail du « pinceau volant » du canto XII, que tout est effacé, que ce monde fictionnel dans son intégrité bascule dans le néant et qu'il ne reste en fin de compte que le procès de la recherche » (150).

novel embodies a critique of words through painting and music. If Virgulius, or his alter ego the « Pinceau volant », produces a book, it exists not only in words, but in fragments, and pictures. The correspondence of Françoise is furthest from the truth, for it has no « correspondances »; it is self-serving to the point of solipsism, turning within rather than connecting with the Other.

This first of Bouraoui's works clearly recognizable as a novel is highly experimental, and as open-ended as Virgulius's flight. The succeeding novels all start anew, on different voyages, are all strikingly different, generating a new form each time. Yet together with the innovation there is continuity in the female presence, embodied first in the enigmatic, silent Koï, who will lead to more solid, expressive, active heroines who begin increasingly to interrogate a male narratology, and even to take over from it: Zitouna, Françoise/Hatshepsut, Twylla Blue, Héloïse.

Hédi
BOURAOUI
Retour à Thyna
l'Or du Temps

II

Retour à Thyna : A Female Epic?

Title

Hédi Bouraoui's *Retour à Thyna* (1995, 1997) is an extraordinary novel, for want of a better term, but it really breaks all the rules of the genre. Henry James once said that the novel is truer to its form "in proportion as it strains, or tends to burst, with a latent extravagance, its mould", and therefore its future is unlimited ("Preface", *PL* 7).

If *Bangkok Blues* is based on an exploration of the culture of the Far East, *Retour à Thyna* is a return to origins which ends with its beginning, the *conte* of the founding of Sfax (the Roman Tafarura, from the Berber "tafrura" "fortifications") told by Al-Fdaoui, paradoxically the murderer/accidental executioner of Kateb, the writer-*trublion*-"shit-disturber", whose violent death, a fall from the ramparts of Borj Ennar, is the puzzle to be decrypted, decoded in the course of the work. The "detectives" are his friends, his alter ego and heir, the journalist Mansour ("the victorious one"), and his cousin and intended bride whom he has raped when she was fifteen, Zitouna ("the olive" or "olive tree"). The concept of "twinning", or doubling, the characters continues, but whereas Koï embodied « l'Autre », the Other, Zitouna is, in the phrase of Évelyne Sullerot, « l'autre semblable », the similar other (as all women are to all men). Not only are the heroines alter egos of the male protagonists, they are also "twinned" with their own sisters, Koï with the reckless Joy, Zitouna with the mercurial Ahlem. By the same token, Virgulius is doubled by the *homme moyen sensuel*

Pierre Blinduel, and the chaste Mansour by the dissipated poet Kateb. Virgulius is a citizen of the world, who has lived on three continents, Africa, Europe, and North America, whereas Mansour refuses to move to France, unlike many of his contemporaries, and never travels beyond Tunis. The "roots" he returns to are not geographical, but temporal, for he revisits the ancient city of Taparura.

Zitouna is in a sense what the text is all about. She is both subject of the epic and its literal and symbolic source. At the same time she functions as the epic hero/ine who creates, or recreates, the dream of the ideal city. She identifies with Thyna, or the Latin Thaenae, « Thyna, ville romaine en ruine près de Aïn Fallat... » (32). Aïn Fallat is the country retreat for Zitouna, and it is the site of the profitable olive groves. Zitouna's permanant home is Picville, a southern suburb of Sfax (south of the Médina, the old Arab walled city), while Mansour lives in Moulinville, a suburb north of the Médina. Living in Picville, Zitouna is closest to the southern countryside of Aïn Fallat. Her name, Zitouna, also sounds very like Thyna, or Thaenae,[1] and her character represents a postmodernist variation on the age-old identification of woman with country, the *mère-patrie*, or, here, the *mère-ville*. This identification has been exemplified in one way or another, for instance, by Willa Cather's Antonia Shimerda in *My Antonia* (1918), Scott Fitzgerald's "fresh green breast of the New World" suggested by both of his female characters, Daisy Buchanan and Myrtle Wilson, in *The Great Gatsby* (1925), and, closer to Zitouna, Kateb Yacine's Nedjma in the novel of the same name (1956). But Bouraoui's is a radical revisioning of this woman as trope for the country. Zitouna is an active heroine with a mind of her own who refuses to be a passive Muse, or object of worship. If she does not tell her own story, she does recount and interpret the tale written by Kateb and left as his heritage. She is at the very least the ideal reader or ideal critic, and the most forceful promoter of Kateb's « écrits », or writings. Moreover, as the narrative proceeds, there are indications that she increasingly finds her own voice.

Structure: « coïncée entre géographie et histoire »

We are told that Taparura/Sfax, capital of the south of Tunisia and center of commerce, is « coincée entre géographie et histoire » (65). But Sfax's geography is its history, and the converse. The walled rectangular Médina, with its seven gates (mystic number – seven days of creation?) and grande Mosquée, is surrounded by the European city (Christians and Jews), the Bled Essouri, with its church and synagogues. Françoise Naudillon

---

[1] In his « Épilogue » to *Retour à Thyna*, François Bruzzo also suggests that *"Zitouna - Thyna"* is an anagram (221). I had not yet read the Epilogue when I noticed the echo.

suggests that the gates represent « les sept piliers de la sagesse » (157), and Dorra Chammam suggests either « les sept péchés capitaux » or « les sept étapes qui mènent à la lumière » (n.p.).

Seven of the ten sections, or chapters, of the novel take their titles and locations from the seven gates: Bab Ed-Diwane, the principal gate, the Porte du Conseil « qui s'ouvrait sur la mer » (18), or more loosely, of poetry (*Diwan*); Bab Bhar, the Porte de la Mer or, more loosely, the modern city, Bled Essouri or the French town; Bab Jebli, the gate to the countryside, closed by the French in 1881 to prevent the flight of the Tunisian rebels; Bab El Farh, nearest the Marché Central, where Zitouna recounts the tale of Kateb; Bab El-Kasbah, where Zitouna wants a cultural center bringing home their past to the commercially-minded Taparurians, whereas Kateb wanted it to become a literary café like Les Deux Magots in Paris, where he could give readings and publicize his writings; Bab El-Garbi, the gate to the West, that ambiguous site of success, or of exile and alienation; and Bab Echargui, « cette porte au Levant qui débouche sur la route de la capitale » (153). Section VIII, however, incorporates the real « Retour à Thyna », where the love of Mansour and Zitouna finally finds expression, isolated from the patriarchy, the ruling powers and their politics.

Of the other three sections, IV, « La Route d'Agareb », uses the movement of Hédi Faker's statue away from the center of town to the countryside as a trope for all the ills of post-independence enumerated at the beginning of the section: the departure of the « colons », the French colonizers, and, in a movement from public to private, Kateb's death, and the future of this nation « coincée entre histoire et géographie » (65). Section IX, "Borj Ennar", is the site of Kateb's death, « L'Innocence sacrifiée ». Section X, the Conclusion, brings us back to Zitouna, « Sur les Traces de l'Olivier ». Significantly, it brings Mansour, who has been working in Tunis, back to Thyna/Zitouna, in a kind of return of the prodigal son. And Zitouna breaks totally with patriarchal tradition, as she has done by enacting and telling Kateb's tale in the Marché Central, by proposing to Mansour, and « La Paix [est] dans les cœurs » (65; 191).

It is important to remember that gates not only permit penetration into the walled city, but also are openings to the outside world. To the East is the Mediterranean Sea, over which all the successive conquerors and colonizers of Tunisia have come, from the Phoenicians in ancient times, who founded Carthage and may have first imported the business mentality – they were the merchants and traders of the ancient world – the Romans, the Arabs, the Norman prince Roger de Sicile, again the Arabs when Abdel el-Moumène « la rendit à l'Islam » (173), the Spanish in the sixteenth century, then the Ottoman Empire, then a period of piracy in the seventeenth and eighteenth centuries « jusqu'au traité du Bardo » (173), then the French in 1881 until the 1950s, when the action of the novel begins, though for the most part it takes place *after* independence (1956), therefore in the '60s and '70s. Robert Elbaz quotes this entire passage to prove that this is a « roman véritablement historique », though he claims that it oscillates « entre l'autobiographique et l'historique » (143). Because « la capitale du Sud ... se fait une réputation dans les activités lucratives du commerce sans trop se soucier de son héritage culturel » (173), Kateb and, later, Mansour and others insist upon « ce retour sur soi, la traversée du désert du temps » (173).

Map of the Novel

The structure of the novel is identical with the map of Sfax/Taparura. It breaks with the linear, sequential narrative of the traditional novel, and adopts instead a circular pattern: in its end is its beginning, to paraphrase the Bible. A similar *apparent* circularity was already at work in *Bangkok Blues*, as we have seen. Following the plan of the circular Médina and surrounding European town, the narrative moves cyclically, between the two pillars of Kateb's tale of the sultan's son who is ultimately killed for his abuse of innocence and virginity, performed by Kateb's adored "victim", Zitouna; and the variant on the traditional tale of the founding of Sfax/Taparura recounted by the sinister Al-Fdaoui in which a sultan (presumably) tries to escape a dreamed-of attack on him by fleeing Kairouan, the then-capital, and pretending to be a workman in Thyna. He is slapped in the face during a ceremony of circumcision for attempting to offer more wealth to the child's family than a workman could conceivably possess. Returning to Kairouan, he gathers his army and completely levels Thyna – surely an overreaction, as the narrative voice drolly comments. The sultan then moves the inhabitants of Thyna to a new site which is to become Taparura, or at least its center, the walled city of the Médina. Two crafty Thynaeans, father and son, contrive to steal two gates from Kairouan, in partial compensation for the destruction of their home, and install them at Taparura. So Taparura is already partly constructed of the remains of the Roman Thyna.

"The Personal is the Political": Feminist Motto

The feminist motto that "The personal is the political" fits this text like a glove, and Bouraoui moves easily back and forth between the love story of Kateb/Zitouna/Mansour and the love of Kateb, Zitouna, and Mansour for Taparura, and for its ancient forerunner Thyna. There is a strong identification, in other words, between the locale and the individual characters. Thyna was discovered buried under layers of sand. By the same token, the characters are layered or masked, whether for good or evil. The layers must be stripped, the masks removed. Mansour's mask is shyness, reserve, covering deep passion, Zitouna's an ambiguity rooted in the secret of her violation which she has kept so long. Kateb's public role as voice of social conscience is betrayed by his private debauchery.

A. La Médina

The Médina is « *la* Médina » and is indeed seen in female terms. Images of sexual penetration proliferate on both the public and private levels. The Médina is a kind of womb. It is « enceinte » – surrounded, but also pregnant – by « *le* sour » (masculine), the fortifications. Bouraoui makes the analogy explicit when he writes of the desire to « ramener l'esprit de Thyna dans l'enceinte même de la médina à laquelle elle appartient » (163). The image is close to that of the *hortus clusus* in the medieval Court of Love tradition. Bab El-Kasbah is viewed as « le lieu idéal pour accueillir la ville-mère dans le sein de la ville-fille... Pour redevenir un foetus, Thyna a dû mourir symboliquement » (163-4). Indeed, the novel is replete with womb/tomb images, alternating births, deaths, and rebirths or resurrections. Zitouna experiences a spiritual death as a result of her violation (and defloration), but she awakens, paradoxically, to a new, liberated self. She is, in fact, both liberated and liberating of all the social strictures, reinforced by ritual, which prohibit sexual activity before, or outside of, marriage. Kateb dies physically but is, arguably, resurrected in the person of his victim Zitouna and his friend Mansour who both endeavor to separate the value of the writings from the messy real life of the author. As D. H. Lawrence wrote, "Never trust the author, trust the tale" (13).

B. La Mer, la Mère, et la Pieuvre

The map image of Taparura is « sous forme d'une pieuvre aux tentacules plongeant dans les jardins, les oliveraies, les villages et le désert » (65). Bouraoui has pointed out that the head of the octopus is Sfax, which also corresponds to the circle of the old city, surrounded by walls with the seven gates leading to the outside. The octopus is a fitting image for a people who derive both their triumphs and their « catastrophes » from the sea: « La famille, la terre et la mer sont leurs trois sources fondamentales » (165). These sources all represent a feminine principle, connecting, suggestively, the octopus and womb images: the earth is a mother; the sea in French, « la mer », is usually equated with the mother, « la mère »: and the mother is the very center and heart of the family. When Kateb dies, his body is found with his head turned towards the sea, a metaphorical return to the womb, which suggests that he has indeed willed his own death, and his feet towards the Médina, as if he were fleeing the rigid and oppressive traditions of the past. Perhaps he can only escape them in death, repair the schism between his public rebellion and his private internalization of patriarchal evils which he manifests in his sex life and various addictions.

Significantly, it is the woman, Zitouna, who does not reject the past as monolithic, but seeks a return to an even earlier past, to origins and sources, while divesting herself of the oppressive structures of the patriarchy. It is no accident that she is a descendant of the Berbers, who are probably the earliest peoples traceable in the Maghreb, before the Arab invasions. Zitouna's coloring, radiant blonde hair and olive-green eyes, reflects this background[2]. In the Berber tradition, women are equal to men and rule the family. It is, in fact, the woman who chooses her mate and proposes to him; Zitouna is recalling this egalitarian past in proposing to Mansour.

The octopus, « la pieuvre », like the sea, is feminine;[3] it comes from the sea, and, moreover, it is a delicacy when beaten tender and served to the family. (The « bastonnade » of the child Mansour by the French schoolteacher, on his father's orders, echoes the octopus ritual: the child is beaten until "tender", and solaced only by his mother's love. [24]) The octopus is thus linked with all the food rituals associated with the major sacred and ceremonial events of the novel: circumcisions, weddings, and funerals. It is the object, in fact, of a ritual within a larger ritual, and is an expression of community values and aspirations. The weddings on the human level subtend a mythic « Mariage permanent entre terre et mer qui intensifie leur passion pour leur cité »... (134).

But the octopus also has some negative implications, for its tentacles reach out in a greedy abuse of power and authority. The government is likened to a swollen octopus, in Zitouna's eyes. The tentacles also destroy the purity of the countryside, polluting and infecting the environment: « Les tentacules avalant, par grosses bouchées, tout l'espace vert, se plantent dans le cœur d'un passé prestigieux de plus en plus empoisonné » (163).

Fragmentation and Integration: Towards Transculturalism

Circularity in a narrative, as in a geographical space, is frequently described as either female or Oriental; here it is a little bit of both. There

---

[2] According to one theory, the Berbers may have intermarried with Crusaders who remained in the Maghreb, further suggesting a multicultural, multi-religious background. Tunisia has the smallest proportion of Berbers at 10%, Algeria at 30%, and Morocco, which has mountains where the Berbers tend to gravitate, at 60%.

[3] There is, however, a masculine noun for it, « le poulpe », but it seems to me Bouraoui more often uses the feminine noun.

is no Aristotelian beginning, middle, and end; there is in fact no closure. We are tending towards a marriage at the end, of Zitouna and Mansour, and towards a reaffirmation of what is to be treasured in the distant past, but the novel ends, as it begins, *in medias res*: « Jet de pierres »... (11). In some ways the narrative strategies are postmodernist – a mystery which is ultimately unsolvable; masquerading, carnivalesque characters à la Bakhtin, an interrogation of history by fiction, etc. – but as a whole it is not postmodernist because it is teleological. It uses fragmentation, but invites integration – on the part of Zitouna and Mansour, but also, most importantly, on the part of the reader. *Retour à Thyna* is intensely self-reflexive: it reflects not only on the uses and abuses of the past, but also on the role of the writer in heightening our awareness of where we have been, and where we may be going in the coming millenium. Bouraoui is eager to transcend the personal and *locally* political in a vision best described, in his own terms, as "transcultural", that is, transcending single cultures by building bridges between them.[4]

The opening epigraph is by Saint Augustine, – himself a Maghrebian born, and a Christian – from *The City of God*, the dream of an ideal city: « Citoyens de la seule cité terrestre dont le règne est l'unique but de tous les efforts, que pouvaient-ils aimer sinon la gloire? » The epigraph sets the tone for Zitouna's, and later Mansour's quest for an ideal, natural city of the past, Thyna.

Epic: The Ideal City

This quest to found – or refound – an ideal, or nearly ideal city suggests that the model for this narrative, which is avowedly of a *genre mixte* – incorporating elements of lyric poetry, journal, confessional, reportage, history, detective story (*roman policier*) – is above all the epic, about the founding – or in this case, refounding – of a city-state. A couple of epigrams drawn from the Tunisian epic, *La Geste Hilalienne*, translated by Lucienne Saâda, point in this direction. But Virgil's *Aeneid*, in particular, springs to mind, a Roman model as Thyna was a Roman city. On his way to found Rome, Aeneas is distracted by Dido, the Phoenician queen who founded the city of Carthage, whose site still remains near Tunis. Homer's Ulysses was also detoured and tempted on the Isle of the Lotus-Eaters, probably the modern island of Djerba in Tunisia, so both epic heroes, the Greek Ulysses and the Trojan Aeneas, are distracted by women in what is now modern Tunisia.

[4] Bouraoui defines "Transculturalism" in his texts, *Créaculture I* and *II* and in *The Canadian Alternative*.

But *Retour à Thyna*, as a self-reflexive, very self-conscious narrative, revisions and interrogates the epic/quest form. It also incorporates tales from the oral tradition – the epic, it is important to remember, began as tales told orally – documents, and letters, from the early eighteenth-century epistolary form of the novel, as clues – notably Ahlem's furious letter to Kateb and his inflammatory reply to a woman whose counterpart in Kateb's tale is *Ahlem Ennar* ("dream of fire") – and whose hair is flaming red; this reply may help to trigger his death.

In the epic, women are generally victims – or doormats, more flatteringly known as "warrior's playthings". They are there either to tempt the hero and be abandoned by him, like Dido, or to watch from the sidelines and applaud, like Aude in the *Chanson de Roland*, the French *chanson de geste*, who simply crumples and dies on learning of Roland's heroic death.

Zitouna refuses the role of victim. Yes, she is violated, victimized by Kateb, but she rises above her victimization, promotes and interprets his writings, and breaks with patriarchal structures which dictate, for instance, blood as public proof of the bride's virginity on the wedding night. Not for Zitouna this part of the marriage ritual, nor, presumably, the orgiastic feastings and collections of material offerings to which Fathia submits when she marries Sadok, Mansour's and Kateb's friend.

A Female Hero?

Is Zitouna herself, perhaps, the epic hero rewritten as epic heroine? Certainly, Bouraoui raises the possibility. She is the active partner in the couple Mansour/Zitouna, and hers is the dream of a resurrected Thyna within the walls of the Médina, near Bab El-Kasbah. The epic hero/heroine must descend into hell, as all three of our principals do. The epic hero, like Zitouna, does not tell his/her own tale. There is a kind of push-pull between Zitouna's forging her own identity, and the attempts of all the males – and to a certain extent, the females – to construct her according to their own needs and desires. The three potential "villains", Tahar, Sadok, and Dahak, are all, to a greater or lesser degree, in love with her. These three are contrasted to the triad/trinity of principals, Kateb, Mansour, and Zitouna. Zitouna is also one of three sisters, so trinities proliferate.[5]

---

[5] Robert Elbaz sees the characters as « des personnages-idées », and stresses that they are not « ronds » (presumably E.M. Forster's distinction between "flat" and "round" characters) (148). Françoise Naudillon, on the other hand, sees them as psychologically complex: « Bouraoui excelle à peindre ces personnages avec les délicates nuances d'un portraitiste. Au delà des caractérisations nécessaires à la fiction... l'écrivain refuse toute caricature et s'offre des développements d'une grande finesse sur la psychologie de ses personnages » (156). I agree with Naudillon, and would say that it is possible to represent both ideas and psychology. But it is up to the reader to re-create the psychology from the clues given.

If Zitouna is not the primordial female artist, she is at least the decoder. She asks. « Quel est le sens caché du conte? » (105). She recognizes that there is « la matière à décrypter » (105). Zitouna, like Mansour, is in the role of detective trying to uncover the reasons for Kateb's murder (?)/suicide (?). She recognizes her sister Ahlem's name in Kateb's posthumous text and begins to piece together the jigsaw puzzle. Did he want, she wonders, to « indiquer une piste »? (106)[6]. If Kateb has mixed myth, oneiric vision, the fantasmagoric with fiction, while Mansour is a journalist who deals with facts, Zitouna tries to bridge the gap between the fantastic and the factual. She is the most active force in reconstituting Kateb's story and its significance. The possibility of viewing *Retour à Thyna* as a female quest novel remains enticing and seductive.[7]

---

[6] On a first reading, one might think that Zitouna was responsible for the marginal scribblings in Kateb's conte, this text « noirci de surcharges, des notes éparses, de commentaires décousus, de fragments de pensée inondant même les marges » (106). It is somehat disappointing to realize that the scribbles are, of course, Kateb's own editing and revisions, discordant and hallucinatory.

[7] There are suggestive resemblances to another twentieth-century re-visioning of the quest narrative, though still in masculine terms, and that is F. Scott Fitzgerald's *The Great Gatsby* (1925), whom many have seen as the archetypal American hero. The title imparts an epic dimension to Gatsby's quest for the so-called "American Dream", which involves a transcendence of class and immigrant status to attain a myth he mistakenly identifies with the shallow Daisy Buchanan. (American literature, too, is in a sense a postcolonial discourse and has afforded models for emerging nations in the twentieth century.) Kateb's and Mansour's quest for cultural integration and identity is hampered by the deformations effected first by French colonization, and later, after independence, by a revolution coopted by the bourgeoisie. Daisy Buchanan, however, could never herself be a questor; she is not even a worthy object of the quest. But Zitouna is in quest of a Tunisian "Dream", for want of a better term, the dream of Thyna. Both novels are structured according to a « retour aux sources ». The ending of *Gatsby* evokes the enchantment of the Dutch sailors who first saw the "fresh, green breast of the new world" (182). *Retour à Thyna*, similarly, ends with the legend of the destruction of Thyna and the creation of Taparura/Sfax.

Gatsby dies in a swimming pool on a raft tracing a circle of blood, comparable to Phlebas the Phoenician in Eliot's *The Waste Land* (1922), who "was once handsome and tall as you", who dies in a whirlpool, sometimes seen as a symbol of the cyclical, and by extension of resurrection. The water imagery suggests a hope for renewed fertility in Gatsby's Valley of Ashes. If there is resurrection for him, it is through Nick Carraway who comes to share his vision, and to tell the tale ("carraway" is a seed, in keeping with the fertility imagery). Kateb, very possibly himself a descendant of the Phoenicians, falls (or is pushed) off a tower, with his head towards the sea, the great mother, not towards the arid desert. If there is immortality, it is through Mansour, who lives to tell the tale, but also through Zitouna, who disseminates Kateb's writings. Gatsby dies at the end of his novel, Kateb at the beginning

"Triangular Desire": Mansour, Kateb, Zitouna

The three principal characters – Mansour, Kateb, and Zitouna – represent what René Girard has called "triangular desire" (*Mensonge poétique et vérité romanesque*)[8]. Moreover, their experiences of violence and fragmentation ae parallel. Kateb's death results in part from violence associated with sexuality and his rape of Zitouna. His funeral, like his sister's wedding, is a traditional ceremony, with one important exception: « C'est elle [Zitouna] qui a tout organisé » (72). The women, contrary to tradition, join the procession unveiled. She is rebellious, then, in regard to the ceremonies we witness.

Even the quiet Mansour knows what it is to experience a quasi-sexual violation: his father has encouraged the schoolmaster to strap him (the « bastonnade ») for going to the circus instead of to school. He has committed « l'erreur d'enfreindre l'ordre paternel » (24). The French schoolmaster is a sadist who, with the complicity of the father, derives sexual satisfaction from this act: « ... plus ses larmes coulent, plus le tortionnaire s'adonne à sa symbolique pénétration » (23), an allusion also to the complicity of the bourgeoisie with the occupying French. Thus, Mansour knows firsthand what it is like to be in the "female" position of powerlessness, as Kateb does when, as a child, he is circumcised by his uncle, Zitouna's father, against his will.

This image of violation, penetration is repeated with relation to the country, moving between the personal and the political: « ... son histoire [est] fissurée par l'Histoire » (12), as Zitouna is "fissured" by Kateb. The *literal* fissure is the « fossé » of Scipio Africanus, located near Thyna, which divided the African continent into north and south. Thus, circumcision is equated with defloration, death, the « fossé », alienation or exile.

Although he is a survivor, unlike Kateb, could Mansour ever take charge without Zitouna, effect a return to origins in order to come to terms with the present and build a better future? His passivity forces Zitouna to become the aggressor in their relationship: does she test him, is it a « test imposé du dedans à Zitouna pour pousser Mansour à sortir de son mutisme et de sa réserve? » (112). Significantly, she challenges him immediately after she has adopted the male role as conteur of Kateb's posthumous tale. At the conclusion of her « performance », after she becomes dizzy and falls, she goes to Mansour « pour le nommer, par le geste, héros du jour » (112).

---

[8] As we have seen, there are other triads/trinities in the narrative, the three potential suspects in Kateb's death, Tahar, Sadok, and Dahak, and, on the female side, Zitouna is the oldest of three sisters; the youngest, Ahlem, is another potential suspect in Kateb's death. Is transculturalism meeting transreligion through the mystic numbers?

Zitouna, however, seems to be the *female* hero of that day, but she is also the "Namer", another term for the Poet.

Mansour is, for the most part, the central consciousness, in the Jamesian sense. He is also both alter ego and heir to Kateb, whose disturbed personality provokes an early death. But Mansour is a survivor. Both Kateb and Mansour are verbal artists, the former a Baudelairean romantic, seeking poetry in excess, the fantastic, addiction, "trips" « n'importe où hors du monde ». The ultimate "trip" is death. Mansour, on the other hand, is a journalist who strives to achieve distance from his material. The two modes of fantasy and realism interpenetrate after Kateb's death.

When we first meet the teenaged Mansour, he sees himself as *not* « un roseau flexible » (echo of Pascal) bowing to the French presence. Sadok flees to his home, the isles of Kerkennah, Tahar – soon to be a prosperous businessman – characteristically flees to Tunis, and Dahak – soon to become an actor – takes refuge near the gate of the Theatre. Mansour, on the other hand, escapes to the Médina, to his friend Kateb's.

"Mansour" means victorious, "Hachem" timid, so he contains contradictions. He is very susceptible to female influences, largely as a result of mother love, « la chaleur maternelle ». She represents an « Amour inconditionnel sans la moindre trace d'affectation », and he has been spoiled (15). The softness of Mansour's mother's love is sharply contrasted to the paternal tyranny, both of his own father and of Zitouna's father with Kateb. There is, in fact, a strongly feminine side to Mansour, which makes him a fitting partner for Zitouna, who assumes some so-called "masculine" attributes in rebelling against the traditional female condition in her world. What we may have at the end, in fact, is an androgynous couple, whose "feminine" and "masculine" traits complement each other.

Mansour meets Zitouna for the first time at her cousin/supposed fiancé Kateb's house, and immediately falls in love with her. Mansour barricades himself, typically, behind books and reads of distant lands, instead of contending with Kateb for Zitouna (22). He becomes a journalist (taking refuge in facts?) and continues to love Kateb, « de toute l'ambiguïté de son cœur » (26).

If Mansour rejects the patriarchy, it is by cultivating a personality and sensitivity that will never tyrannize over others: « Rares sont ceux qui possèdent la force de s'effacer pour laisser briller les autres prêts à éblouir les incrédules et les innocents » (135). Mansour is not aggressive, not a conqueror, save of himself (135). Rejecting the patriarchy necessarily implies rejecting Taparurian materialism. He prefers « l'art du verbe » to « celui de thésauriser l'argent » (138). Words, not money, are to become the new "currency" in Mansour's world. Mansour's passivity strengthens the role of the heroine. And she may prefer Mansour to Kateb for his very malleability: strong heroines may not need strength from their men, but rather sensitivity.

Mansour's family, in Moulinville, lives at a crossroads « de deux routes, l'une menant vers la gare et la ville européenne, et l'autre vers Bab El-Jebli et la Médina » (139). This location is perhaps a sign of Mansour's entrapment, in which he must choose which road to follow – or neither. His first meeting alone with Zitouna, significantly, occurs in neither the European/French nor the Arab setting, but in the ruins of the old Roman town of Thyna. Zitouna urges him to « consacrer un article à l'origine et à la splendeur de cet endroit sacré qui lui tient à cœur » (157). She sees that Mansour's weapon will be words, not physical violence.

Kateb is a continuous presence in their lives. If he has written the script which they perform, it is characteristically fluid and ambiguous, asking more questions than it answers. It is up to Mansour and Zitouna not only to decrypt or decode it, but to face the consequences. These three, we are constantly reminded, along with the marginalized Amar and Moshé, « n'ont jamais trempé leurs mains dans l'eau bourbeuse des gains et du crime » (173-4). On Thursday, the « jour des morts » (Holy Thursday?), Mansour visits Kateb's grave, on the road to Gabès, murmuring a few verses of poetry by Aboûl Hassan Sahnoûn: « Il y a en moi un tel désir de Toi/que si la pierre le supportait/Elle serait fendue/Comme par un feu violent » (180). He is thinking both of Zitouna, and of Kateb in his tomb. The split rock sounds like an echo of Christ's resurrection when the disciples go to his tomb and find the rock rolled away, the body gone, possibly referring to Kateb's resurrection through Mansour and Zitouna. But the split rock could also refer to the « violations » of Zitouna, Mansour, and Kateb (as well as to the fossé of Scipio Africanus). The « feu violent » could refer to Ahlem, whose name appears in Kateb's tale as Ahlem *Ennar*, meaning fire, which is also the name of the site of Kateb's death. At Sadok's wedding Mansour has learned from Amar that Ahlem sent a letter to Kateb: « Cette nuit-là, je lui ai apporté un couffin de figues et une lettre d'Ahlem, la sœur de Zitouna » (112). Suspicions begin to arise that Kateb has committed a kind of suicide, using Ahlem as an instrument by inciting her to kill him in order to avenge her sister's honor. When Ahlem drowns by swimming out to sea, Mansour « se sent vide comme une coquille remplie de sable sans la pulsation de l'eau nécessaire à sa survie » (186). The water undoubtedly serves a symbolic function as well; Kateb died with his head towards the sea, and all invasions came from the sea. Moreover, Kateb's tale concerns a fisherman – suggesting St. Peter, the fisher of men, and also the rock, "petros", on which Christ founded his Church. Mansour tells Sadok he is trying to explore the links between Kateb's tale, *L'Ogre et les trois filles du pêcheur*, and that of the origins of Sfax/Taparura (183). Thus, the imagery of the novel derives from multiple religions, as well as diverse cultures.

While Zitouna mourns her dead sister, Mansour is obliged « de quitter sa ville natale et la femme qu'il aime » for Tunis (193). Would Kateb have simply stood his ground? Mansour's heart remains in Taparura, and he refuses to join the "brain drain", turning down « une mission journalistique en France » because he remains « un simple citoyen attaché à son patrimoine régional » (199). At the end, he rediscovers « enfin sa sfaxitude ! » (207).

During his absence, Zitouna has continued to plan the installation of a theater and museum in the heart of the Médina. And when the prodigal son returns, it is Zitouna who proposes to him, as she has previously singled him out as the hero of the day when she performed Kateb's tale: « C'est moi qui te demande en mariage, rompant ainsi avec les sacrosaintes traditions » (209).

___Kateb is in a way the other side of the coin from Mansour. Almost the first thing we learn about him is that he smokes and drinks, and that he does not practice what he preaches: « Kateb va jusqu'à défendre la cause féminine et sa libération des traditions: Pure démagogie puisqu'il est incapable d'appliquer ses théories dans sa propre vie » (30). Although we are told that he resembles Mansour and Zitouna in keeping his hands clean, he seems to belong to the same camp as others with good intentions, such as the Combattant Suprême (based on Habib Bourguiba), who end up abusing power. His very personality is *fissuré*: between public and private, between « La ville arabe et la ville européenne » (39), between past and present. He is a reformer who cannot reform himself. He wants to abolish Ramadan fasting, the repudiation of wives, and the serving of alcohol in public places after 8 P.M. (42). It is hinted that these proposed reforms may lead to his death. In reality, ironically, he is a womanizer, a rapist, and an addict. Perhaps this fissure in his character accounts for the cryptic nature of his verbal art: « Je ne peux m'exprimer que par l'indéchiffrable ! » Mansour replies, « Non, c'est ta conduite qui est ambiguë » (31). His writing, like his self, is torn between two worlds, "the eunuchs of Cairo" and « les superduperies des élucubrations » of Paris, giving him an inferiority complex « en dépit de ses ancêtres prestigieux comme Apulée, Saint Augustin, Ibn Khaldoun et tant d'autres... » (37). He complains of the sickness of literature in his country, both in the national language and in French (37). In despair, he hangs his « poèmes-fruits » from trees, symbolically giving them back to nature in protest against the lack of modes of production and distribution.

His funeral rites are described in great detail. The body is provided with scissors so that « le Diable ne vienne pas perturber son âme » (43). Kateb's soul seems restless even after death: « Le corps ... semble s'animer par les secousses de transport », again supporting the theme of resurrection (50).

Only in his absence, and with the aid of his writings, do his motives begin to be unraveled by the others, and by the reader. It is pure speculation whether his rape of Zitouna is in part motivated by revenge against her father. Once Kateb has raped her, however, he has possessed her virginity, thereby usurping the role of "husband" in the marriage ritual. Kateb attacks the Taparurian « rentabilité », materialism of Si Mokhtar and other patriarchs (118). He seeks to heal the fissure, to bridge the gap, to « abolir les frontières entre la vie et la mort, le passé et le présent, le rêve et la réalité » (118). But he is himself split. Perhaps only his death, and Mansour's and Zitouna's inheritance of his vision, will restore wholeness. We are told that, from the point of view of the community, « ... l'erreur de Kateb, justement, c'est d'avoir poursuivi le non-lucratif » (66). Ironically, in his posthumous tale recounted by Zitouna, *L'Ogre et les filles du pêcheur*, the eldest sister, Zarzour Aâkal, says to her father, « une bouchée dans le ventre et une bouchée dans la muraille », stressing food as the necessary of life (95). The middle sister says, « une étoile dans les habits et une étoile dans le tapis » (96)[9]. The youngest, Ahlem Ennar, stresses money and food: « un dinar pour manger et un dinar pour combattre les dangers » (96).

Is Kateb's death a kind of triumph?[10] We are told, « Le sublime pour Kateb ne consistait pas à avoir goûté le fruit défendu ou à l'avoir gâché avant sa maturité, mais à s'installer sur le bord du rempart entre deux creneaux pour fumer sa pipe et rêver aux étoiles par les nuits sans lune » (186-7). He dies, in fact, by starlight, perhaps with the complicity of the real Ahlem, and thinking of his « étoile », Zitouna.

If Zitouna is the very heart and soul of the novel, her sister Ahlem is almost equally fascinating – in some ways more so. Perhaps the two represent the positive and negative of female artistry, as Mansour and Kateb may represent the positive and negative of male artistry. The two women can be seen as doubles, as can the two men, but there is also a cross-gender pairing of similar personalities: Zitouna and Mansour, Ahlem and Kateb. Zitouna writes nothing, but there is a crucial exchange of letters between Ahlem and Kateb, which both help to solve the mystery and add to it. Mansour finds an anonymous note, torn to bits, probably from Ahlem, in Kateb's tobacco pouch after his death: « ... certaines des imprécations qu'elle contient sont celles que Kateb a reprises et griffonnées en marginalia sur le

---

[9] This seems to be the only non-material wish, perhaps an echo of Kateb Yacine's *Nedjma*, the star.

[10] Robert Elbaz sees Kateb as a kind of « bouc émissaire », car un sacrifice est nécessaire au maintien de l'ordre nouveau » (146). While I agree that Kateb's death is a kind of sacrifice, I think he is more than a scapegoat for others, that he chooses his own death to restore order to himself, and not to the society he abominates.

texte du conte » (188). Pieced together, the note reads, « Ma sœur n'est plus la même. Je ne la reconnais plus. Nous l'avons tous perdue » (188). Ahlem deplores Zitouna's defloration as if it had altered her value utterly. The note reveals a number of aspects of Ahlem: she is more traditional than her sister if she accepts that a rape turns Zitouna into a different person, and that the different person is somehow lacking all the positive qualities of the old Zitouna. Losing her virginity by force is no shame at all; Zitouna is a victim, not a fallen woman, except according to the most literalist interpretation of virtue. Perhaps, in fact, her value has increased, and the new, resurrected Zitouna is better, arguably, than the *jeune fille*, the blank page, who was « salie », as Ahlem puts it, by Kateb. Ahlem's note is fragmented and has to be reassembled, rendered coherent, like Kateb's poèmes-fruits hung from trees and at the mercy of wind, and passers-by.

Kateb has written a provocative reply to Ahlem: « *Ogresse* de malheur, que fais-tu? » This is an allusion to the tale, but unclear: « ... il enrobait ses idées d'obscurantisme et d'ambiguïté » (187). He advises Ahlem to be kinder to herself than he has been to himself: « Instaure le rêve [her name] si tu peux ... dans la vie ... dans la vie... Pas le désastre que je n'ai pu éviter dans la mienne! » (187). Kateb, it seems, recognizes a kindred spirit in Ahlem: they are both dreamers, fantasists; they are both out of control, hotheads, firebrands; they are both, ultimately, responsible for their own deaths – a "suicide" which may be a provoked manslaughter, and a "suicide" which could be an accidental drowning. Ironically, even in their deaths they are circumscribed by tradition, suicide being a mortal sin in their, as in so many, religions, so it is made to look like something else. Furthermore, in addressing her as the Ogress of the tale, he is blurring her identity, since she is also the Ahlem Ennar of the tale who kills the Ogress and rescues her sister. Kateb seems to be suggesting that Ahlem is both accomplice and victim in her own fate[11].

If the more rational, moderate, calmer Mansour is Kateb's heir, then Zitouna is Ahlem's. Ahlem's is a "Death by Water" like that of Phlebas the Phoenician in *The Waste Land.* The *flame* of Ahlem is symbolically extinguished by water. If hers is indeed a suicide, it is an active one, to swim out to the point of no return, like Kate Chopin's Edna Pontellier in *The Awakening* (1899). She does not put rocks in her pocket, like Virginia Woolf, or iron weights, like Faulkner's Quentin Compson, and walk into a river. And as in Chopin, *The Waste Land*, *The Great Gatsby*, and *The Sound and the Fury* (1929), water is also a symbol for the resurrection.

[11] It is also unclear to what extent Ahlem's suicide is triggered by her jealousy of the middle sister Ibtisem.

As Mansour does with Kateb, Zitouna is constantly warning Ahlem to listen to the voice of reason. She recognizes that Ahlem « *s'enflammait* pour rien » (181; emphasis mine), and counsels her to remember only Kateb's writing: « ... il a mis l'accent sur le *bien collectif* dans son œuvre, même s'il a été atrocement égoïste sur le plan personnel »... (181). In the final analysis, Kateb's and Ahlem's inability to escape tradition leads to their deaths. Zitouna, on the other hand, is to be an instrument of healing and salvation through her ability to come to terms with the past, accept it, and transcend it.

Zitouna may be predisposed towards liberation by her Berber heritage, but above all by her identification with the olive, and the olive tree. Her eyes are olive green (13). The olive tree is not only the national symbol, but it is « l'huile d'olive », as Mansour remarks, « qui nourrit, illumine, et guérit » (168). Does Zitouna, then, represent nourishment, healing, light? The Zarzour of the tale, Zitouna's fictive self, urges her father to keep food in the bin, and a food ritual is attached to each of the major ceremonies of life and death. When Zitouna "baptizes", or anoints, Mansour, after reciting Kateb's tale, it is with a mixture « savamment dosé d'huile, d'extrait de fleur d'oranger et de jus de citron » (101). The oil, one assumes, is olive oil, and it is a healing « baume miraculeux qui l'apaise sur-le-champ comme il l'a fait sur le cuisant de la bastonnade enfantine ... »(101), when it was his mother who comforted him. François Bruzzo puns (perhaps excessively) on « *ma-terre-(n)elle* », linking Zitouna with the mother country: « ... elle, Zitouna, en son corps, en ce savoir de son corps, science de femme, savoir *ma-terre-(n)elle*, qui porte hors de soi, qui parle certes mais qui en dit plus qu'elle n'en sait et dont le dire et le nom excèdent le savoir: *Zitouna* dit en son nom qu'elle est *retour à Thyna* » (222). The association is prepared in Mansour's mind by his close relationship with his own mother.

The olive oil also lights lamps, and Zitouna provides illumination for the others to look into their hearts and souls. Last but not least, the olive branch is an almost universal symbol for peace, as in the United Nations logo. For all of her activity – she leads a women's demonstration pictured in *Paris-Match*, like Chraïbi's liberated "mother" in *La Civilisation, Ma Mère!* (1972) – in the final analysis she is a peacemaker. As in Chraïbi and in Rachid Boudjedra's *La Répudiation* (1969), we witness an alliance of women and young poets in the Maghreb.

The question then arises, is Zitouna not herself a poet? If not, why not? Though this is not a first-person narrative, we are usually well aware of Mansour's point of view, but more likely to be surprised by Zitouna's, presented mainly through actions and words. Presumably she makes speeches of her own, not those scripted by others.

Fire images link the two sisters. Like Ahlem, who is a redhead, Zitouna is associated with fire. She is « d'une chevelure solaire et d'yeux alguemarine » (174) – sun and sea – an odd description of a blonde. And oil lights fire and lamps. She is the "virgin oil" slipping between our fingers. She has suffered her "Paradise Lost" at the age of fifteen, has passed through hell, and emerges to « son paradis retrouvé, Thyna » (73). If she is the « symbole de la femme par excellence » (80), she is linked with nature: stars, sun, sea, air, fire. « Les hommes poursuivent leurs intrigues », we are told, while the women enjoy nature (68). She is fascinated by the cartouche at the pool in Thyna, « Amour chevauchant un dauphin » (55), again a water image. And she arrives from the sea to recite Kateb's tale, like Botticelli's Venus rising from the waves.

Zitouna is not only the olive, but the « Inaccessible étoile » (13), an allusion to Kateb Yacine's *Nedjma*, and « cette perle berbere » (14). Even if the tale she recites is scripted by Kateb, she flouts tradition in performing and interpreting it in public as a female conteur, and is implicitly contrasted to the male conteur, Al-Fdaoui, who may have been Kateb's executioner, intentionally or not. But Zitouna is also « la romaine Thyna vêtue à la tunisienne qui s'avance en personne jusqu'au cœur du marché de la Taparura moderne ... » (94) – an image of Art in the Marketplace. There are hints of her finding her own voice: the contrasting interpretations by Zitouna and Mansour of the mosaic of the « lionne et chevaux » are suggestive of their characters. She identifies with the « lionne » which, though victorious, will always « chasse seule », while the male goats forever outnumber her – a critique of "male bonding" to the detriment of the female? She reacts strongly « aux non-sens et aux âneries sur les femmes » (136). In fact, Zitouna is often mentor to Mansour.[12]

Zitouna is also an amateur archaeologist, in the crucial dialogue at Thyna in Chapter VIII with Mansour. Like the Roman mosaics, Thyna/Taparura represents a kind of cultural mosaic: « ... ici le brassage des races et des religions a été plus tolérant et plus convivial que chez eux... Quant à nous, nous n'avons exclu personne ! » (161). Mansour exclaims, « C'est pour cela que je t'aime, Zitouna » (161). At Thyna, Zitouna « a le sentiment d'avoir retrouvé sa virginité » in an almost mystical moment (164). Her wound is healed, which has been « l'écho de la déchirure du pays et de leur ville » (163).

---

[12] Françoise Naudillon notes that Zitouna « symbolise la femme arabe moderne, éduquée, militante et lucide, qui a son mot à dire dans la gestion du pays ». She adds, « Les femmes mieux que les hommes pour conduire les destinées du pays... L'idée est suggérée », and notes that in addition to Zitouna, we have « Fathia, sœur de Kateb et épouse de Sadok, qui s'avère aussi une redoutable femme d'affaires » (156). However, it seems to me that Fathia is, in fact, wedding the "man's world" of her husband, whereas Zitouna is forging her own destiny – and that of Mansour as well.

Perhaps Zitouna, finally, has found her voice, and it is the voice of Thyna. She becomes a female artist by forging her own path: « Elle ne récite plus de formules apprises, mais crée elle-même les notes de son chant pour mieux les transmettre » (164).

Ahlem's death delays the formation of this androgynous couple, but it is also the catalyst for solving – insofar as possible – the mystery of Kateb's death. Mansour and Zitouna have much in common: « ... ils ont vécu dans le cocon double d'une famille traditionnelle versant vers un modernisme taillé à sa mesure, et de l'autre, d'une banlieue taparurienne hétéroclite où les races et les religions vivaient en harmonie » (181).

Although they will become a couple, there is no closure to the novel, which will continue like life itself. Those who could not escape the past – Kateb and Ahlem – were destined to be the sacrificial lambs, permitting a resurrection of Mansour and Zitouna who will value the past without being imprisoned by it. Thus, at the end, Thyna itself, the ville romaine, is reborn in the womb of the old Arab town, the Médina (212). As Mansour says, there are three things that remain: « les mosaïques de Thyna, l'avenir de Taparura et la vigueur de l'olivier » – past and future, works of man and nature. And Mansour will not regurgitate Kateb's writing, but find his own way through Zitouna: « Je me sens vivre en toi ... rien qu'à travers toi » (211).

The narrative voice of the opening and closing phrases sounds depersonalized, representing neither the point of view of the characters, nor of the novelist-as-historian who informs the beginning of each chapter. The « Jet de pierres » of the opening puts us *in medias res*, in an eternal present. The « jet de pierres » anticipates the usually empty stone fountain that replaces not only the French colonial presence the rocks are being thrown at, but also a whole transitory series of leaders and political movements. The ending is prophetic – no matter what changes, the olive tree, personified in the novel by Zitouna – remains an eternal presence, a symbol of resurrection in ever-recurring spring, or life radiating out of death in a Whitmanian rebirth: « S'en vient le jour de ta gloire, Zitouna ! » And the novel could "not-end" with these words: « à continuer... ».

Hédi BOURAOUI
LA PHARAONE
ROMAN
l'Or du Temps

III

La Pharaone :

A Female Visionary

If *Retour à Thyna* could end « à continuer », Hédi Bouraoui's third novel, *La Pharaone* (1998), is in a sense a continuation, but also a backwards movement, beyond the Roman period to the very origins of civilization in ancient Egypt. Like *Bangkok Blues*, the novel explores both a distant past and a distant place, where the protagonist/sometime narrator finds himself in an alien setting and, especially in *La Pharaone*, in a strange and unfamiliar time. As in the two previous novels, there are double heroines, but one is present, one past, one Occidental, one Oriental. If they are related in any sense, unlike Koï/Joy and Zitouna/Ahlem, it is as "sisters under the skin".

La Pharaone, like *Retour à Thyna*, is an ambiguous quest, involving five or six people, whose end is inevitable yet, at the same time, completely enigmatic. The title character, La Pharaone, pervades the text, but tells her own story only at the end. It is a striking example of Bouraoui's narratological shifts into the female mind. Here a dead woman speaks – or does she? In the earlier *Retour à Thyna* (1996; second edition 1997), the heroine, Zitouna, who embodies, as her name suggests, both the ancient Roman town of Thyna and the mother country, post-independence Tunisia, finds her own voice and speaks not only for the liberation of her country, but also of all women.

But why Hatchepsut? The ancient Queen of Egypt, the only female Pharaoh (unless one counts the much later Cleopatra) was perhaps the first modern woman – though there were doubtless other contenders, notably the mythical Biblical Eve. A recent television documentary on Hatchepsut calls her "The Queen Who Would be King", a title borrowed from Kipling's novel and the Michael Caine-Sean Connery film, "The Man Who Would be King". Not bisexual except in a spiritual sense, but rather androgynous (like Zitouna who usurps the male role of talespinner or Fdaoui, and like the CN Tower, later), she donned the Pharaoh's garb, bare-breasted and all, after the death of her useless husband Thutmose II. While she had to wear the garb of a warrior king to validate her claim to suprem-acy, she was a wife and mother and, evidently, later the passionate mate of her scribe (or architect, as some historians would have it) Senmut. Bouraoui explains the ambiguity: the two Senmuts were brothers, and adopted the ruse to protect the Queen's reputation – and their own heads. The television documentary suggests evidence that Hatchepsut's body, which has never with any certainty been identified, is buried in a tomb adjacent to that of her commoner lover with whom, of course, she could not be buried.

But this is to get ahead of the story, always a temptation considering Bouraoui's deliberately tangled narrative structures, analogous to a detective story (as is *Retour à Thyna*). The characters are the linchpins, but their narratives overflow like the Nile itself, spilling its banks and inundating them with fertility, but also bringing mysterious deaths, including those of one of the contemporary characters, Rahmane, and we learn later – or do we? – of Barka, the leading male contemporary character, and of Senmut himself. The language has the lushness and exuberance of the Nile valley, surrounded by harsh desert sands, but also by *les roses des sables* (another Bouraoui title). At times the characters, ancient and modern, sound alike, in contrast to the shifts from classical storytelling to contemporary slang in *Retour à Thyna*. But both work towards a fusion of ancient and modern, of time and space.

La Pharaone is, above all, a love story, of the ancient world, the modern, and the future. This scaffolding enhances the curious overlapping of the three principal pairs of lovers, who become confused one with the other. It is best to subsume the discussion of female narratology, for the moment, to that of the love patterning. And finally we end with perhaps two, or even three, female narrators, not one. The three couples are, of course,

- the long-dead but still vital Hatchepsut and Senmut;
- the young lovers Ayman the Copt, and Imane the Moslem student. It is no accident that their names sound alike, almost rhyme. They are a Romeo and Juliet separated by the culture and tradition of the Moslem patriarchy, yet bound together as Copts and Moslems are by their land. Their child will embody the hope of the future, though that future is apparently fertilized by his grandfather Rahmane's apparently ritualistic, sacrificial death. Imane metamorphoses constantly into a new Hatchepsut, from the point of view of the central consciousness, Barka Bousiris. But is she also Imeni, the Pount princess who triggers Hatchepsut's jealousy and the eventual murder of Senmut/Kabar, the scribe's real name?
- Barka Bousiris ("Barka" is an anagram for "Kabar") and Francine, the French mistress of both his youth and present, form the third, more mature couple of the present day, but there are *glissements, intermittances du cœeur* between Imane and Barka, and finally an elision of Francine and Hatchepsut. Is it Francine who simply edits the words of the dead Barka, or does she also interpret and create, in fact become Hatchepsut?

Ayman and Imane: « L'Amour Continue »

Imane and Ayman, the first of the couples we encounter in the text, are also the youngest and "purest", in the sense of inexperienced. It is their love which is destined to continue on this earth, through their son Nisr.

But it is important to remember that they are, at least in part, the constructs of Barka Bousiris, the « scribe-voyageur », or modern version of the wandering minstrel, or troubadour. He serves as a go-between for the young lovers, which advances the plot, even playing the role of Ayman's father at their wedding. If Barka is the principal narrator/observer in the Ayman-Imane plot, he is the principal actor in the other two love stories, between himself and Francine, and between himself as the resurrected Senmut/Kabar and Hatchepsut.

The young couple, « au coude du Nil », also introduce the river as timebinder, culture-binder, gender-bender. Ayman is a hotel keeper beside the Nile, the center of civilization. He is a Copt whose name, Ayman, literally means faith, and we are told « Ayman c'est la foi du Nil » (17). Imane's name is the feminine version of her husband's, and also means faith, but her faith is Islam. Her father, representative of the patriarchy, is named Rahmane, or "one who gives grace", one of the attributes of God. Despite the spiritual conflicts between and among them, the common denominator is faith, but one which is shaken to its root, and probably destroyed in Rahmane. All three names seem to echo also the German "man", "one", and the English "man", "humankind". There is perhaps also an echo of "manna" from heaven, which descends on the young, while the older men are destroyed.

As the Nile divides the land of Egypt in half while also uniting it, the lovers are both divided and joined by two faiths which have one root. The word "copti" itself is a « forme arabisée qui désigne à la fois l'habitant et le pays » (15). The Nile « partage le pays en deux, saignée aqueuse », a "no man's land", which could be an echo of Gilbert and Gubar's book, *No Man's Land.* If so, is what we are witnessing a "woman's land", a space inhabited by women? The Nile is a « fleuve magique et divin » (15) with which Hatchepsut is identified, « la Déesse-Pharaone, Hatchepsout, qui a capté *l'imaginaire* de ce monde » (16; emphasis mine), infusing it with her own artistic spirit. It is also the cradle of the « *nourritures terrestres,*[1] mentales, artistiques et scientifiques de tout un continent ». It resembles « un Dieu dérouté qui ne reconnaît jamais la limite de ses forces » (16). If the river is "a strong brown god" (T. S. Eliot's *The Dry Salvages*), it is equally a goddess, the « mère de l'Univers », or "Oum Kalthoum" (102; 162): « Mère de l'Univers où tout doit aboutir et repartir dans une rythmique sans cesse à révéler... » (21). Her caves shelter the lovers when Imane leaves her father's home. Barka recognizes in Imane's cave that of the ancient Egyptian Senmut/Kabar (157). The Nile also represents measureless time, or history.

Ayman is a peasant's son, adaptable, willing to change and accept everyone: « ... il semble épouser l'efficacité même de l'Occident rêvé ». He meets, in the course of his work, to paraphrase Herman Melville's *Moby Dick* (1851), a kind of "Anacharsis Klootz deputation from all the nations of the world", coming from the river. This couple finds itself « face à l'Histoire et la Modernité », divided and yet united by the river, which separates the two banks, yet « l'amour coule entre » (22).

Despite its superficial resemblance to the classic story of fated young lovers trapped between warring families, Shakespeare's *Romeo and Juliet*, these lovers are destined not only to survive, but, in the words of William

---

[1] The reference is to the work of André Gide.

Faulkner, to prevail. It is the older lovers who fit into the love-death theme, definitively described by Denis de Rougemont in *L'Amour à l'Occident* (*Love in the Western World*) (1940), where the only total fusion occurs through death.

Imane physically resembles the female Pharaoh, « cette beauté-echo de la Pharaone », but is capable of accepting a new love. Ayman is struck by her likeness to Hatchepsut, « son profil finement ciselé, ... ses yeux en amande, larges océans ténébreux et mystérieux, imprégnés de la densité d'un passé prestigieux... » (20). Imane is a scholar, possibly in search of herself; after her early commitment to studying feminist writers, she ultimately becomes rector of l'Université El-Azhar (196), a secular and intellectual "ruler" as Hatchepsut was a religious and national one.

Towards the end of the first chapter the « scribe-voyageur » (or presumed narrator) finally introduces himself: « Et me voici, moi Barka Bousiris, maître de cette tache d'huile longitudinale qui s'étale, fertile et nourricière, dans un désert infini et angoissant » (22). Anchored to his own hieroglyphic origins, he invents his quest as the camel carries its own hump (157). His simile inevitably recalls the old saying, « Le chameau ne voit pas sa bosse », perhaps indicating Barka's vain attempts to reject his fate. Barka seems to be the outside narrator but, like Lockwood in Emily Brontë's *Wuthering Heights* – the great-grandmother of all convoluted narratives, before Henry James, before Joseph Conrad and James Joyce – the story doesn't end with him. His narrative is framed by the "tale" of Francine, as well as by a letter from Imane, followed by the writings of the Pharaoh herself. Hence the secret at the heart of the text is a transformation from a seemingly male to a female narrative.

Barka traces the condition of women in a Moslem patriarchy back through Imane to her mother Amira and her grandmother. Amira rebelled against her grandmother's way of life and chose her own husband. But she in turn is jealous of her daughter Imane's greater freedom: « ... elle reste cloîtrée dans son mutisme sans promesses et sans pleurs. Imane la croit tranquille, rassurée » (42). Yet, like the dry Egyptian clouds, she is capable of the rain that brings fertility, or destruction. The Nile delta is a familiar symbol of fertility, specifically of the female genitalia, the "delta de haute sensualité » (43). Amira's jealousy and anger at her husband may be transposed to her furious, obsessive son Béchir. Imane's virginity is compared to textuality; she is a blank page which life will inscribe (46), in contrast to her mother, who is bitter about the way in which life has inscribed her.

Before union can be accomplished, the father must be sacrificed. Imane must enact in a sense a female version of the Oedipus complex: to liberate oneself by killing the father. Not that Imane, consciously or unconsciously, wills her father's death, but her rebellion against the patriarchy, her escape from the paternal home, signal her father's decline and ultimate demise. The instrument may be her brother Béchir, but she provides the catalyst.

Rahmane, or "he who gives grace", an apparently godlike figure, is ultimately the one who loses, first grace, then his life. He opposes Ayman's courtship of his daughter because, supposedly, he prefers a more suitable match, but the young man's Christianity is clearly an issue. Rahmane is a free thinker, « libre-penseur », up to a point, but both father and daughter have internalized their faith, while rejecting the fanatical « Frères musulmans » (38).

When Imane leaves her family, she tells her new confidante, the French Francine, that she fears she has lost both lover (to Margaret Lee, the facile Canadian) and parents. She hides in the pyramids of Giza where her father is the caretaker, in a kind of Ali Baba's cave linking Arabic with ancient Egyptian mythology (62). As Barka asks, « qui possède le courage de cohabiter avec les morts ? » (63). The answer, of course, is not only Imane but himself, as he proceeds to an italicized flashback to Hatchepsut's world, « *à l'image d'Isis ou d'Imane* » (63). The ancient buried woman comments on the modern: « *Je suis le Verbe ... Je rends la chair à la mort pour indéfinir la vie* ! » (63). Is it Barka or Hatchepsut who speaks? Or both? Thutmose III, her nephew/successor, seized his own power by writing over the female Pharaoh's history on the Sphinx, which is falling into ruins, ambiguously male or female, and missing its nose which scents reality. Thutmose, a warrior where Hatchepsut was a peacemaker, knew that « *s'il le désensable ... il sera Roi* » (64). Barka's mission is to « *Rétablir la véracité de cette scribaturie imposée par le furieux Toutmosis III sur le poitrail de ma Princesse... Pourquoi violer l'exemple unique de puissance féminine ? Quels sont les traîtres qui ont subverti ou tué son impact ?* » (64). But in the final analysis it is the women surrounding Barka who rewrite *male* history.

The enigmatic Sphinx poses two riddles focusing on a cobra. Ayman answers the first two as « la belle turquoise de la vie qui reprend ses droits » (67). The Sphinx then poses a third riddle, « galet qui jalonne le cours du fleuve-écriture », reminding us again that the river symbolizes writing, or hieroglyphics to be deciphered. Barka sees the "first truth"of the Sphinx as a return to original innocence, so that to understand death is to understand life, and come full circle.

Imane in turn drifts among the living dead (65), among « des lambeaux de momies, des fragments de sculptures, des bijoux rouillés, des déchets indéfinissables, bref, une caverne... » (77). All this must remain hidden lest Rahmane be fired for professional incompetence. The rumor spreads that Ayman has kidnapped Imane. Rahmane's plans for vengeance are as ill-conceived as the response of the nations surprised by the Six Day War. Hatchepsut creates this new love of « le couple aux religions inversées »; it is they who will "make love, not war" (unlike their religions) (79). Barka makes it clear that love, or a kind of communion, equals writing. Rahmane's death echoes that of the sick Fisher King in T.S. Eliot's "The Waste Land": "The Fisher King is dead". It reenacts the age-old ritual of the death of the father which empowers the son. But first he disappears, like his daughter, « sans laisser de traces » (99). At first Imane fears he has been dismissed from his position. She also remembers that he had said, « Je ne donnerai ta main qu'à celui qui t'aimera comme moi ! » (99). Imane cannot mourn him, not knowing his fate: « Ce n'est pas lui qui est mort, c'est son nom ! » (101). The emphasis is always on text, and the Poet is the Namer. Rahmane is absent, like an ancient Pharaoh, and his name becomes « Wala Haga, *M. Personne* [Mr. Nobody], un rien de rien ».

Barka draws an analogy between Imane's quest for the father's name and that of the goddess Isis for the name of the father of all the gods, « le père lumière ». By magical means she creates a serpent from the god Râ's own saliva – shades of DNA! He fails to recognize it as himself because it is the only animal he has not created. When it stings him, Isis conjures him to reveal his "Secret Name" in order to cure him, and he answers: « Je suis Khepri au matin, Râ à midi, Atoun le soir » (101). But she insists on the secret name, not the known ones, and in desperation he divulges it to her in a whisper. The first syllable of Rah/mane's name sounds like Râ, and Barka tries to help Imane « déchiffrer un seul mot qui ressemble à: 'foi'..., 'à la fois'..., 'foi'... » (102). Imane has simultaneously lost her father and found her future husband. If the secret name is "faith", in losing his name, the implication is that Rahmane loses his faith.

Rahmane wanders in a « *no man's land* des oubliettes » that Imane refuses, but she nonetheless feels partly responsible for the fate of this now child-like father, fallen from his pedestal, wandering in rags in the wilderness, like a latter-day King Lear on the heath. According to this scenario, Imane plays the role of the blunt-spoken but true-hearted Cordelia. But he tries to chase her from his dead man's city. Rahmane's Lear-like soliloquy reveals truth in madness:

> *Qui m'a volé ma fille ?... Qui ? Ayman, ce vaurien ou Barka, ce revenant ? Moi, le condamné ? Le Pharaon moribond des âmes ? Farouk, Nasser, Sadat ? ... La perle de mes yeux ? ... Ô, vent, féconde ce Nil qui coule dans mon sang... Je suis Wala Haga ... Serpents me piquent... Sang et désert... On va chercher la mort... Viens...* (117-18)

In this soliloquy, recorded by Barka, possibly edited by Francine, Rahmane metamorphoses into Barka/Kabar, lover of Hatchepsut, and past and present merge. The serpent's sting evokes the race memory of the serpent that stung Râ, in a kind of Jungian collective unconscious, and that tempted Adam and Eve in the Garden of Eden, as well as the cobra of the Sphinx's riddles. As the ancient Egyptian myth reveals, the serpent is blood of our blood, flesh of our flesh, and evil is within mankind.

Oddly enough, only Betty, Margaret's rebellious daughter, is able to reach Rahmane. His wife Amira asks jealously, « Pourquoi a-t-il fallu une étrangère pour le ramener au sein de ma propre famille ? » Barka compares her question to Hatchepsut's: « Pourquoi un homme de famille modeste peut-il me servir mieux qu'un pharaon ? » (118). If Imane represents tradition, Betty represents « aisance ». Rahmane rediscovered is described as a « revenant », an epithet he himself applied to Barka (118).

Rahmane is found only to be lost again, this time to literal death when he intervenes as a mediator between political rioters and the police. He becomes thus a kind of "sacrificial goat", but his death is a mere statistic, outside of his own family. Barka, significantly, learns of Rahmane's death when he leaves the Cairo Museum, where he has been marvelling at Hatchepsut's statue with the missing nose, « tellement distinct de celui de Toutmosis III empâté, étalant ses narines comme une tente du désert » (120). Hatchepsut's mummy has never been retrieved, or at least identified, so the statue is the closest Barka can get to her. If, in the museum, Barka inspects piles of archaeological relics, Rahmane's death is reduced to « une trouvaille archéologique sans note explicative » (122) – but Barka is to supply, in imagination, that note. Rahmane's death prefigures Barka's, with whom he is in many ways identified: « Une partie de moi vient de mourir. Je me revois dans l'aura de cet homme loyal... » (123).

Barka's earlier dialogue with Rahmane, in fact, gave him the impression of a soliloquy (123). Barka warns him, as the Fool warns Lear, « Chercher un sens à tout, c'est de la folie ! » Rahmane admits, « Je suis peut-être fou ... J'ai toujours voulu poursuivre l'Éternité ». Barka warns him that « L'éternité ... n'est à posséder par personne », but his obsession with Hatchepsut manifests his own drive to possess eternal love – that of Tristan and Isolde, of Romeo and Juliet. Barka admits he seeks eternity himself through writing, « juste pour sentir son frisson, le temps d'un éclair ... et puis, c'est la mort ! » He adds, « Tu vois, c'est toujours cet obélisque sacré qu'il faut bander pour scribe-voyager l'amourir au Ciel... » (124). He thus prophesies the manner of his own death.

Barka admits that Rahmane's was a difficult, dark personality, perverse like still water. His body is rendered, torn apart, thrown into the Nile, like Kabar's, perhaps like Barka's, Kabar's reincarnation – though in the latter case the body itself seems to vanish into thin air. As in the French New Novel, such as Robbe-Grillet's *Les Gommes,* everything is called into question. The reader, trying to put in order his impressions, is constantly *dérouté,* put off guard by the narrative surprises Barka (or Francine?) has in store. Rahmane's death, like Barka's, also recapitulates the haunting image of Kateb the writer, executed and thrown from the battlements in the earlier novel, *Retour à Thyna.*

The mystery is not solved, but intensified, by the autopsy, which discovers that Rahmane was killed by a policeman's bullet, then torn apart, perhaps by a mob (139). His body is not like the mummy of Ramses II, that other exponent of male dominance, but must be pieced together, and cannot enter the underground kingdom of Osiris. During the course of the reconstitution, they discover that he has been castrated, deprived of the ultimate male symbol of power. The death of the Father seems to Barka to explain the castration (146). His death has permitted others to flourish: it has « donné naissance à l'amour de Béchir pour Betty, semé l'espoir d'un retour à la source du pays dans le cœur d'Ayman, et d'un mariage possible avec Imane » (147).

It is Béchir, not Imane, who, like Oedipus, displaces the father, to the point of going mad. He assumes his father's authority with his elder sister: « ... je suis le mâle de la famille » (152). The two young people with almost identical names represent the "yin and yang", the animus and anima in psychological terms.

Barka compares the impact of the death of the father on Imane and, aeons ago, on his love, Hatchepsut, who lost Amon and Thutmose (159). Appropriately, for their wedding, the young couple choose a historic setting, Sidi Abdel Kader north of Aswan. They are carried to the site by the feluccas which seem to cleave the Nile, in a sexual image of penetration. The surrounding islands display « leur corporalité amoureuse, ... comme une peinture impressionniste ... » (162). The description evokes the Song of Solomon, with its heady scent of tropical flowers, and bird song. Although the marriage, at Imane's behest, follows Islamic ritual, there is also an echo of Christ on Palm Sunday in the figure of a « pèlerin perdu » on a donkey, pursued by the music. In the person of the Nubian boatman, the text prefigures the expedition to Pount ordered by Hatchepsut, and described at the end of the novel in her journal. The wedding is not only that of the young couple, and of past and present, but also of three major world religions. It cuts across all boundaries of class, time, and religion, as Hatchepsut tried to do.

Ayman's and Imane's wedding night takes place on board the Seti Ier. The consummation of their love is signaled by the completion of the statue of Hatchepsut: Ayman's father found the sculpted nose in his field, gives it to Ayman as a wedding present, and Ayman gives it to Barka, permitting his « réunion inattendue avec ma Déesse » (168). The modern-day wedding leads to their recovery of their heritage. Throughout the wedding night Barka evokes the legend of Osiris, the god torn to bits and then made whole again by the goddess Isis. Passion itself becomes a religion, as « leurs chairs ... finalement se miraclent... ».

The second part of the novel, much briefer than the first, begins with the birth of Ayman's and Imane's first child, born (by their choice) near Philaé, another site of origins, sacred to Isis who avenged her father, Osiris. Philaé was also the place of strongest resistance to Christianity, where the cult of Isis rules, a cult of words, and therefore of female authorship:

> Le temple fut d'abord érigé pendant la trentième dynastie pour célébrer le culte d'Isis. Ses longs portiques et sa silhouette gracieuse offrent aujourd'hui son visage *livresque* au soleil et aux étoiles. Voyage ouvert comme une <u>épitaphe</u> au passage du Nil, *flots de mots* [note the internal rhyme] qui naviguent dans *le chapitre* du fleuve... (186; emphasis mine)

The firstborn is a son, but they show no gender bias; they decide on a cognate name if it is a daughter, Nisra or Nisr. Chapter XV, in which Nisr is born, is entitled « Nilomètre du naître ... disparaître ... » (185), suggesting Sartrean existentialism: Being and Nothingness, « L'Être et le Néant ». The pun is on « naître » – « n'être », or, as Hamlet put it, "To be or not to be, that is the question".

Imane is Isis giving birth to Horus the Falcon. She is also the Mother of the Universe (194). She and Ayman want to go beyond words, to the Word made Flesh, beyond the « cartes perforées du tendre » of the twentieth century (as opposed to the « Carte du Tendre » of the seventeenth-century romance). Imane's reflections on Nisr predict his future leadership: « ... *Il ira à l'école de Luxor, pour être* Ras el Omma ! [Tête de la Nation] » (194). Thus Imane is seen as a female poet who creates in the verbal sense as well as the biological. Her song is validated by a fakir's horoscope: « Votre fils sera souple, prévoyant, susceptible et très déterminé. Il connaîtra ses buts et s'y dirigera avec force et discipline... Sans difficulté, il vaincra les autres qui accepteront volontiers ses idées » (194-5). Nisr is presented, in fact, as a kind of Messiah, reinforcing the Madonna symbolism attached to Imane, who is both a Mary and an Isis. The Marian worship of the Middle Ages came close to making the Virgin into a mother goddess of the ancient cults (from which the idea of the Virgin does descend). God speaks to Imane about Nisr: « *L'héritier légitime de la foi, ce fils-espoir des destins de la cité et des lois, saura embrasser toutes les croyances* » (195).

Imane creates the name "Nisr" as she has created the baby (195). This chapter of birth climaxes with Imane's prayer: « *O Dieu, regardez et protégez Nisr !* » (196). The name is a cognate of "Misr", the country, Egypt, but also Cairo.

Béchir, thinking Ayman a false convert, is blinded by violence and shoots him in the right shoulder at the very moment that Ayman was coming to tell Barka of the imminent return of the Hatchepsut Sphinx to the Cairo Museum, so the destinies of Ayman and Barka remain intertwined (198-9). As Ayman puts it, « À mon avis, il a voulu nous punir, Barka et moi » (199). It is Betty, once again, who leads the lost sheep back to the fold, the son Béchir as she has already led the father Rahmane.

Barka: « Le Scribe en écrivoyance »

We are somewhat startled when Barka first introduces himself on page 22, well into the first chapter. Up to this point we have assumed an omniscient author recounting the tale of the young couple « au coude du Nil". Barka's assertion of the « moi » sends us back to the epigraph Francine includes at the beginning of the text, where Barka tries to repudiate the previous epigraph from François Jacob's *La Statue intérieure*, an image recalling Henry Moore's dictum that the statue already exists within the block of stone, waiting only to be freed from it: « *Pas un geste là, pas un mot qui ne soit imposé par la statue intérieure* ». Trying to distance himself from this determinism, Barka claims that his technique is shaped by the oral tradition of the Maghreb, and that he uses the "I" only to impose a kind of continuity on his fragmented narrative, while repudiating its egoism. He tries to create himself in transit, to escape from « ma Statue scribaillante pour mieux scruter le présent et préparer l'avenir ». Yet Barka seems unconsciously to live out a destiny he cannot evade as the ancient Kabar.

Barka admits, in fact, that he is « en mission commandée par un génie intérieur dont j'ignore encore les intentions » (23) – in other words, « La Statue intérieure », which turns out to be the Statue of Hatchepsut, transformed finally into a living, breathing woman. If Nisr is the Word made Flesh, so is Hatchepsut. She is also Galatea brought to life by the sculptor-creator Pygmalion, but in this case she is at least as much the creator of Barka as he is of her. He calls at once upon the "*Om-ed-Dunya*", or Mother of the Universe, who soon becomes identified with Hatchepsut.

In the second chapter, « Scribe en écrivoyance », Barka describes himself as a citizen of the world: « Barka Bousiris de Carthage,[2] de la 'Ville Lumière' [Paris] et de celle que les Iroquois nomment 'Ah, ce qu'il y en a !' [Toronto] » (25). He wishes to sate his « soif du transculturel », defined by the novelist Hédi Bouraoui, Barka's creator and alter ego.

Like Edward Saïd, Barka feels marginalized by the Occident, by the Greco-Roman tradition. The Mother of the Universe, however, is far more ancient, and he wants to translate the Jungian collective unconscious of the whole world, « remonter aux sources de ce que nous sommes » (28). He calls his love "existential", in the sense of man and woman creating his/her own world; « Créaculture » is the central concern in Bouraoui's thinking. In the process, his (Bouraoui's? Barka's?) text breaks the boundaries between epic and novel: « Je suis le Transversant épisodique qui ne cherche pas à meubler sa vie, ... mais à ranimer les pierres et les murs où s'inscrivent les gestes épiques. Là, l'image se fait roman... » (26). Thus, the stone is made flesh and spirit by the power of words.[3]

His narrative begins with a dream of his own mother, who metamorphoses into Hatchepsut, and the Nile itself. Hatchepsut's dying husband, Thutmose II, appears, and Barka dances with the Queen, murmuring « je t'aime » (27). The dream has a Freudian ending, a fall into a well: « Tout se dissipe » (28). The recovery in memory of this ancient love is counterpointed with that of the modern. Barka begins to feel he is leaving his skin « dans ce pays des origines », foreshadowing his fate, when his body is never found, but seems to vanish.

---

[2] Catherine Guillery remarks that Barka's first name evokes the son of Hamilcar Barka, Hannibal, who in turn evokes Carthage battling against imperial Rome.

[3] ... as later in *Ainsi parle la Tour CN*.

Curiously, his first encounter with Hatchepsut occurs in the Occident, in Italy, which – along with London and Paris – has appropriated the ancient treasures of Egypt. This particular treasure is a Sphinx of Hatchepsut, androgynous as was the "Queen Who Would Be King". Barka introduces her in the words of the Italian guide:

> C'est la première femme dirigeante de toute l'humanité.
> D'habitude, elle se fait représenter avec des traits masculins pour convaincre son peuple de sa toute puissance sur le pays. Mais dans cette statue que vous voyez là, c'est la féminité, la finesse, l'élégance, la femme dans toute sa gloire... (29)

But the name on the chest is that of Thutmose III, the nephew. It seems, at any rate, to have been sculpted before she declared herself the Pharaoh.

When Imane accidentally tumbles into the river Nile, Barka sees in her « la statuaire de Hatchepsout, en granit noir, trouvé à Thèbes, mais aujourd'hui propriété du Musée de Rome » (30). The Nile itself (like the river in *Huckleberry Finn*), is a source of myths and legends, hence of language. Ayman initiates Barka with a taste of Nile water, saying, « Tu reviendras en Égypte puisque tu as bu l'eau de son Nil ». In fact, he never leaves Egypt. Barka interprets thus Ayman's prophecy: « *Nil-syntaxe* qui me *transcrit* dans *le lexique* bariolé des croyances et des traditions. Ayman est convaincu de cette *sentence* gravée dans sa mémoire comme *les hiéroglyphes* sur les murs des temples » (30; emphasis mine). Hieroglyphics becomes the archetypal writing that must be decrypted, decoded. And the river presides over it, « malgré sa pollution et ses détritus » (30).

Ayman is a young Barka, as « Imane et Hatchepsout ne seraient peut-être qu'une seule et même personne » (31). At this point we are also introduced to three other principal characters, Francine Castel, « directrice du Centre Culturel du Caire », who will eventually offer Barka's vision to the world; Margaret Lee, his promiscuous traveling companion from Toronto who for a time threatens Imane's relationship with Ayman; and Ibrahim, the mysterious taxi driver who doubles as guide, and is the sole witness to (or is he the perpetrator of?) Barka's death.

Barka's mother was unknowingly responsible for sending him to Egypt to solve the riddle (the Sphinx's?) of the *Omma* (Nation, or Mother Country). Barka explains the omnipresence of the mother:

> Si j'implique ici ma mère, c'est que je sens derrière elle l'invocation présente de Hatchepsout dans cette histoire de couples séparés et

> unis par un destin secret et incompréhensible qui creuse les fossés des oubliettes. (34)

Barka in turn becomes a mentor to Imane, urging her to seek « la liberté qui unit, non celle qui sépare ! » (35), as opposed to having her memory « tatouée par un Islam exacerbé » – an echo of Abdelkébir Khatibi's *La Mémoire tatouée.* Barka has an out-of-body experience: « Je suis le scribe et l'amant réincarné... Imane et Ayman, Hatchepsout et moi » (36). Their « mers émotionnelles » equate the « Mer » and the « Mère ».

Two themes emerge from the permutations and combinations of the three principal couples, ancient and modern: the resurrection, and art, or writing, as the source of that resurrection. It is the artist who, in a Whitmanian sense, serves as timebinder. As a visiting scholar at the University of Cairo, Barka longs for the Renaissance of Egypt, a country which is both fertile and deadly. Like Thyna, or Sfax, of the earlier novel, Cairo resembles an octopus with its « banlieue tentaculaire » (5). Barka explicitly compares the Maghreb, his mother land, the land of the setting sun, to the Machreq, or the East, including Egypt, seen ultimately as the land of the rising sun, or resurrection. He refers to « La Ballade du Ressuscité », hawked by camel drivers, and mentions that even the tourists have the sensation « de naître dans le néant du néant » (57). In the necropolis Ayman and Ibrahim guide students who see a tomb open on two sides « [qui] laisse sortir l'âme et fait ressusciter le corps ». Barka implies the resurrection of Christ, whose « pierre tombale » is rolled away, and whose body, like Barka's, disappears. But this invocation fuses with the existential *L'Être et le Néant*, and William Blake's essentialist "Songs of Innocence": "To see the universe in a grain of sand/and heaven in a wild flower": « L'éternité ne s'inscrit pas seulement dans la pierre tombale qui défie le temps, mais aussi dans les grains de sable qui expose à vue d'œil la néante condition de naître » (58). Both existential and essential, Barka himself becomes « en même temps grain de sable et univers, rejetant derrière moi ... ma société de consommation » (58). Barka puns verbally on the Pharaonic obsession « que Mort s'im[mort]alise ! ... Le refus de mourir définit l'espace pharaonique... » (55).

If Imane cohabits literally with the dead in her hiding place, Barka seeks to cohabit, first figuratively/spiritually, then literally, with the dead Hatchepsut. The Word will be his instrument of resurrection: « *Je viens de renaître Scribe... Je suis le Verbe ... Je rends la chair à la mort pour indéfinir la vie !* » //– « *Je suis ressuscité par l'amour de la Déesse* » (63). The quest for origins is really for a « *vérité première* » (68).

If his mother lies behind his passion for Egypt, his father launched him on his quest. A businessman, he urged his son to subordinate the material universe (as Kateb and Mansour also try to in modern-day Tunisia), and sent him to the « École des livres »:

> – Vois-tu mon fils, en te faisant scribe, tu ne posséderas pas les biens de ce monde, ni la richesse de Carthage, et il n'y aura personne pour commander ou gouverner ta pensée ... sauf l'inspiration. Dans ce domaine tu seras libre car le scribe est toujours son propre chef. (69)

The quest for origins becomes a « quête du Paradis de l'enfance, ce jardin total de l'épanouir » (70). Is it his « Statue intérieure » speaking when he says, « Je ne sais pas que je sais »? (71). His internal voyage resembles the Nile « qui méandre partout » (71). All the characters come together at the Sphinx. In a dream Barka sees a triangular bronze plaque engraved with hieroglyphics. The triangle is the delta, the archetypal female symbol of fertility, but it also suggests René Girard's concept of "triangular desire » (which played so large a part in *Retour à Thyna*), in which love only manifests itself in the face of a third, a rival – which also triggers art. This novel is filled with triangles: Barka-Hatchepsut-Francine, Ayman-Imane-Margaret Lee, Rahmane-Ayman-Imane, Hatchepsut-Senmut-Imeni (princess of Pount). Francine and Hatchepsut, Barka admits, are the « deux femmes de ma vie ». Imane, the Egyptian, is described as « mon Croissant fertile ». Thus the three principal couples are intertwined, « emprisonnés dans des cercles en ellipse » (84).

From Chapter VII we would infer that the childhood paradise was Barka's and Francine's, « notre paradis d'enfance à Bagatelle, premier jardin des enchantements » (87). But Francine also attempted suicide, and, like Hatchepsut, tries to lure Barka into following her in death. Her action is that of Dido, Queen of Carthage, whose lover, Aeneas, abandons her to found the city of Rome. Barka, like Aeneas, refuses to follow, because « Je voudrais encore scribe-voyager libre et dans la joie » (87).

Francine, inviting him to explore the history of Egypt, to go back to « l'Égypte osirienne » (88), both competes and collaborates with Hatchepsut. So he is specifically seeking the origins of art. Born in Carthage, Barka becomes a celebrated international scholar who, like Senmut/Kabar, « dirige les activités de tout le monde » (91). His is « la mémoire transculturelle ». But he never loses his sense of fun, of self-deprecation. Humorously, like a circus ringmaster, he invites his audience: « Venez nombreux écouter la voix royale du passé » (91). Often accused of egotism, he is, in fact, like his father, modest and humble. He distances himself « pour me critiquer et m'ouvrir aux autres » (92).

Barka's worship of the Goddess goes beyond any consequences Francine had anticipated. Describing Hatchepsut in Chapter VI, the narrative « moi » suddenly becomes Kabar, not Barka – the "kâ" in Egypt signifies the life force – and the past becomes present:

> Hatchepsout m'appelle *scribe-speculum*, à l'instar de Senmout, le maître des écrits, son « porte-parole » et, en même temps, majordome de la famille royale:
>
> – Déroule tes papyrus. Lis le livre des secrets. (79)

As Senmut/Kabar/Barka says, « Écouter, c'est aimer ». Love leads to death, and death to life, to « un amourir toujours ressuscité » (83).

Francine, sensing a rival, but mistaking her first for the living Imane, not the dead Hatchepsut, reassures herself, « Il me revient toujours ! » (85). In a very important sense, she is right, for it is Francine finally who translates and transmits the voices not only of Barka/Kabar, but also of Hatchepsut. Francine eventually realizes that her rival is art, not another woman. Paraphrasing Sartre's « L'enfer, c'est les Autres », she says, « L'artiste, c'est l'enfer des autres ! » (95). Barka's retort is in his paradisiac vein: « Au contraire, l'œuvre d'art fait briller le paradis des autres » (96). At one point Francine has cried out in the grip of passion, « Aime-moi pour t'aimer toi-même, mon mal-aimé ! » (82). Her love finally mediates « entre cet univers et celui de l'au-delà ».

The Sphinx is a product of art, but also a self-portrait of the artist. The Sphinx is androgynous, animus and anima in one being, as Ayman and Imane, that prophesied apocalyptic couple, are in two beings. Imane is the third woman in Barka's life, who closely resembles the Sphinx and Hatchepsut: « Et voilà que je viens de rencontrer la Troisième qui va m'ouvrir la porte étroite, Imane, venue là sous le regard parlant du Sphinx ... » (82). « La porte étroite » refers to André Gide's novel of the same name, translated *Strait Is the Gate*, but also to the path to Christendom, so that Barka bridges cultures and religions. And the religion of the Pharaohs was neither Islam nor Christianity.

Barka describes the « Dieu-Nil » as a « source niagarante », thus linking Canada and Egypt (and anticipating *Ainsi Parle la Tour CN*). He further draws an analogy between the Dieu-Nil and Hatchepsut: « En parfait androgyne, il (ou elle ?) arrondit ses seins fermes dans l'arrogance... Se précise ainsi le profil de Hatchepsout... » (83).

Aboul'Hol is the « Sphinx en désagrégation constante... » (64). It is fragmented, like the narrative, or the tangled interrelations of the couples. Barka identifies it with the "Queen Who Would Be King": « Sa tête colossale, d'homme ou de femme ?, dégagée des torrents de sable, étouffe son corps de lion, au beau visage énigmatique dont le nez, décapité par mégarde d'un coup de canon d'un Sultan mamelouk, est allé se faire voir ailleurs... » (64).

If Thutmose III commits sacrilege by erasing her name from the statue now in Bologna, his successor Ramses II committed an even worse desecration. Not content to erase her name, he replaced it with his own, as he did Akhnaton's, her fellow heretic[4]. The treasures found in the arrogant Ramses II's tomb are the richest that have been found. In fact, Barka exonerates Thutmose III of any wrongdoing towards the statue of Hatchepsut, and places the blame squarely on Ramses II, the « Pharaon qui domine l'univers » (94): then, in 1817, « Belzoni triomphe des sables et rend au monde le beau visage de Ramsès et sa gloire, hautement proclamés à Abou Simbel, et que l'adversité des vents a savamment enfouis » (93). Thus an Egyptian Pharaoh has appropriated the work devoted to a female Pharaoh, and European culture in turn has appropriated ancient Egyptian. Ramses, an enemy to all religions but his own, is also the Pharaoh who enslaved the Israelites in Egypt, until Moses was able to lead them forth. It was undoubtedly also the Sphinx of Ramses II that Shelley was thinking of when he wrote his heavily ironic epitaph to worldly glory, "Ozymandias". Two trunks of stone, buried in the desert and crumbling to dust, bear an inscription which concludes, "Look on my works, ye mighty, and despair".

Barka realizes he is treading on dangerous ground, in judging harshly both the all-powerful Pharaoh, and the West, destroyer, colonizer, appropriator of Eastern values. Moreover, he has presumptuously placed the blame on them for the disappearance of the female Pharaoh's nose, and even gives a lecture on « Le nez du Sphinx, et le dilemme de son impact » (90). He knows he can be accused of sacrilege. Even the veiled women will pursue him vengefully for taking the part of a woman who rebelled against orthodoxy. The representatives of orthodoxy in his audience feel he is claiming, perhaps advocating, that « le féminin devient masculin, et le

---

[4] In fact, Akhnaton may have really been androgynous or bisexual, as Hatchepsut only pretended to be.

masculin féminin ». After Hatchepsut, the next feminist movement in Egypt did not occur until the revolution of 1919, at the entrance to the University of Cairo: « Là où Hoda Chaarawi ... immortalise le premier mouvement féministe après la Pharaone ». The sculpture, *L'Éveil de l'Égypte*, by Moukhtar, commemorates this rebellion by creating a stone Isis, who speaks through lips of stone[5] to the Sphinx:

> *– Lève-toi. Libère-nous de l'esclavage des harems et du joug des gouverneurs. Ouvre tes pattes majestueuses, tes yeux de lynx ... Fais-nous découvrir l'au-delà des deltas engloutis dans le marasme des horizons ...* (54)

Barka links the stone Pyramids, as well as the sculpture, with language. He notes that Al-Ahram, the name for the pyramid, is also the title of the greatest newspaper in Cairo. As Isis protects the Sphinx/Hatchepsut, Barka is protected « par le pouvoir magique du scribe » (94).

But one must still ask, why is Barka so fixated on the nose of Hatchepsut's Sphinx? Several clues are given. If it had been transported to England, he fantasizes that it would have scented the Industrial Revolution: « Le nez d'Aboul'Hol a disparu. Il s'en est allé flairer la révolution industrielle au British Museum à Londres » (75). Or, Barka speculates, it could be likened to an accusing finger pointing to the vast culture lag between the Orient and the Occident since the late nineteenth century. The nose by itself is not marketable, but rejects pragmatic materialism. It can be linked to the theme of immigration, the journey undertaken by many compatriots, and their forcible integration into Western culture: « Et qu'est devenu le nez de la statuette de la reine dans sa migration européenne ? » (75). Importantly, it is also compared to the near rupture of Ayman's and Imane's relationship. Ayman and Imane are divided, but united, by a common ancestry: « Tant d'échos millénaires ont poussé Ayman dans la triade christique, et Imane dans le croissant islamique ! Deux branches du même arbre pharaonique... » (76). Barka himself, on the aesthetic level, like the couples on the emotional, seeks an integral vision, a kind of Derridean « plénitude », « *la complétude de mon univers fragmenté* ! » (33). As with the narrative registers, the text is both deliberately fragmented, chaotic, and, on another level, transcendent and unified.

Hatchepsut is haloed by Western as well as Eastern mythology. She is the Sleeping Beauty of Charles Perrault's archetypal French fairy tale, awakened by the magician of words, Champollion, who decodes the

---

[5] ... as will, later, the CN Tower.

hieroglyphics on the Rosetta Stone: Champollion « a réveillé la belle au bois dormant de l'archéologie » (95). As Barka affirms, art translates the incomprehensible – a contradiction in terms. An angry Francine, however, accuses Senmut/Kabar, and, by extension, her own lover Barka of sucking the life out of the loved object: « C'est un amant aveugle, et elle lui a fait confiance ? Il s'en est servi pour sa réussite sociale. Il l'a donc vampirisé, non ? » (95). Francine is obviously here projecting her own victimization onto Hatchepsut, but there is a more than partial truth in what she says: one reading of the Gothic tradition is that the artist battens on others, sucks their life, rather than living to the fullest himself.

Shortly after Barka's controversial lecture on Hatchepsut's nose, Ayman offers Barka the gift of a "Charme Vili", a tiny ebony columnar sculpture with three birds perched on it pecking at a grape. They seem to be looking at the top where a man is seated, cross-legged like a tailor, resembling Rodin's "The Thinker": « C'est un scribe africain perdu, comme moi... » (98). The amulette, which Barka is still wearing at the end, seems to predict his death, and the three birds echo the three couples, the three women, the trinity.

This prophetic Chapter VIII, "Charme Vili: Magie ou Mektoub ? », reflects the dangers incurred by the artist, who must balance the sacred and the profane (98). As Edward Saïd also emphasizes in *The World, the Text, and the Critic*, « le sacré est indubitablement lié au politique et à l'économique » (98). In the midst of all this, sacrificial goats are chosen, and Barka is to be one of these. But, he asks, « Pourquoi et qui veut me tuer ? » (111). The country itself , composed of the delta, seems to be heading towards « une mer dévorante » (111).

Barka projects himself into a picture of Nout, the mother of us all, « femme arquée sensuelle et maternelle » (111). This image of the overarching sky is female, and Barka/Senmut/Kabar relives the ancient expedition to Pount with Hatchepsut. The Vili amulette proves that the expedition was to the African coast, not the Arabian. Hatchepsut and Senmut called the terraces of Deir el-Bahari, « 'Myrrhe de Pount', pays originel des Dieux » (112). From Pount, probably, came the Three Wise Men of the Christian tradition: « L'usage de l'encens dans la tradition judéo-chrétienne remonte aux ancêtres de la reine de Pount » (112). Barka/Kabar speaks of the animosity and gossip generated by his relationship with Hatchepsut. He also built three chapels, again the mystic number, dedicated to the queen, which aroused resentment. « Pourtant », says Barka/Senmut/Kabar, « j'ai bel et bien fait cette expédition à Pount avec

Hatchepsout » (112), an expedition recreated in detail with murals and sound by the Royal Ontario Museum in Toronto.

Kabar's Transmigration into Barka

The end of Barka's quest, his ultimate resting place, is the womb/tomb (164). On the stages of his journey he meets those – like Ayman and Imane – whose race memory helps him piece together the mystery, as well as the Nubian whose ancestors constituted the kingdom of Pount.

Ayman's and Imane's marriage brings forth the missing nose of the Hatchepsut Sphinx, leading to « complétude ». The nose seems to suggest the breath of life, and is connected with images of marriage, birth, and death. In a sense both couples, ancient and modern, consummate their relationships on the wedding night of Ayman and Imane.

At Aswan, the inscrutable Ibrahim leaves Barka near the obelisk, compared to a uterus, the « lieu de rassemblement de culte et de foi » (175). It reflects the sunlight « pour glorifier le Dieu Amon Ra » (175). It also has a « tête explosée », an exploding, teeming womb? – in any event an image of fragmentation. When Barka's goddess appears, he conjures up his « amourir naissant » (176) and addresses her thus: « O toi révolutionnaire aurorale qui a su imposer et confirmer l'amour que tu avais pour ton scribe ».

If the womb equals the tomb, we are looking at the myth of eternal return (177). The caves and tombs where Imane hides give birth to new life, but the stone cavern also suggests the philosopher's stone. Barka proceeds to resume Hatchepsut's life story:

> Toutmosis III, ton beau-fils, se met à te haïr, t'accusant d'être « l'usurpatrice » d'un trône qu'il estime sien ! Hatchepsout, tu instaures ta nouvelle façon de gouverner: tu te fais couronner roi, sans renier la barbiche. Masculinité revendiquée, tu prouves que tu es capable de sophisme politique et de subtilités mythiques afin de légitimer le pouvoir des deux couronnes hautement posées sur ta tête théocratique. (177)

The trait he most admires is her chosen, not natural, androgyny. The two crowns of Egypt reflect this doubleness.

I am reminded of Willa Cather's "Stone Lips" passage in *Death Comes for the Archbishop* (1927), the mysterious murmuring cave/womb/tomb in which the celibate Archbishop is forced to take refuge from a storm, and where he becomes terrified – by the sexual suggestiveness? The obelisk is not only magical and a womb, but specifically the inventor of languages (180); Barka is doubtless thinking of Champollion. Language arises not from birth alone, but from the simultaneity of birth and death (181). Barka writes, « Mes doigts donnent naissance au texte qui balbutie, enfant de ma langue... » (181-2), while Ayman and Imane will have a flesh-and-blood child. Barka recognizes the vocalization of the women, Francine and Imane, who will finally tell *his* story: « Cette verbalisation ... nous relie à la communauté de Hatchepsout... ».

By this point in the novel Barka's identity is increasingly subsumed by that of Senmut/Kabar the scribe, and Francine can only watch her lover being lost to a woman long dead. The climax of the ancient love story occurs on the expedition to Pount, when Hatchepsut was accused of being ambitious and unscrupulous, wanting to make money in an entrepreneurial, capitalist sense. In fact, what she really wanted to do was give away her money for incense of the land of Pount. According to Hatchepsut, her father Amon ordered her to undertake this quest to install « un Pount dans sa demeure céleste » (113). She and Senmut/Kabar wandered together for twenty years without incurring scandal, his devotion to his goddess being unquestioned (114). Francine notes the transformation each time Barka opens his mouth, revealing his « altérité ambiguë » as man of both past and present (114).

Hatchepsut's only daughter Néférouéré died in the eleventh year of her mother's reign (115); Senmut/Kabar had been charged with her education. But the queen does not abandon him until the nineteenth year, three years before her own death. The reason for this abandonment does not become clear until Hatchepsut herself, the female voice, takes over in the journals that form the conclusion. The mystery is read through « les érections d'écriture », a trope connecting sexuality, hieroglyphics, and the art of writing. Increasingly, the novel looks towards death, Barka's being prefigured by Rahmane's. Barka researches the life of his goddess before the final crossing, foreseen like death without knowing the exact moment it will strike (119). As for Hatchepsut's death, she too has effectively disappeared into thin air, as no identifiable mummy has been found – only her Sphinx with the long-missing nose. But we do know what she looked like from the sculpture in room 43 of the Cairo Museum.

The Nile is the source of vitality and creativity, « le fleuve de son encre » (126). We are told that if man is the river, woman is the bridge. But Hatchepsut sought to be both in one. Traditional male and female power are compared, for instance, at Abu Simbel, where the dominant male

Ramses II controls his queen Nefertari: « Au Nord, se faisant plus petite, à l'échelle humaine, Nefertari, l'épouse du pharaon, ose à peine lever le doigt », although she, like Hatchepsut, was nursed by the goddess Hator (127). But Hatchepsut, like Zitouna, refuses to be contained and controlled, and exemplifies female rebellion and creativity. Ramses, the warrior king who silences women, is contrasted to Hatchepsut, the queen of peace who enables men: « C'est le triomphe de la paix sans guerre qui galvanisa Hatchepsout... Que la paix soit ! » (129). Moreover, in death, there is no major distinction between the female Pharaoh's tomb and her lover Kabar's. Barka describes his lifelong quest to safeguard « le patrimoine des sources langagières et culturelles de ma Pharaone » (148).

Written in stone, « inscrit sur la pierre », like the mosaics of Thyna, Barka pursues « une scriberie » irrigating the desert, giving birth to a new alphabet (148). Hatchepsut, in choosing androgyny, fuses male and female creativity, as the androgynous couple, Zitouna and Mansour, have done in the earlier novel. Francine tries to bring Barka back to present-day reality: « Vraiment Barka, tu es pitoyablement amoureux de mythes » (144). But he denies the charge, claiming that he is obsessed not with Hatchepsut as myth, but « parce qu'elle a bouleversé l'ordre des choses » (144). Francine protests, « Je t'ai porté en moi statue de sel frustrée et révoltée, et tu m'as éclaté au visage comme une bombe ! » (145), a reference to Albert Memmi's novel of alienation. But as the novel progresses, Francine increasingly becomes one with the material. When Barka implicitly compares her to Dido of Carthage, and the Egyptian Imane, he addresses « le pays natal et le pays d'accueil, le libéré et le colonisé » 148). All these bipolarities are fused in the bearded, breastplated Hatchepsut and in Barka, that son of Osiris [Bou = son of], destined to be torn apart only to give new life.

If one couple in the present becomes conjoined, another in the past ruptures. And the reasons for that rupture can only be disclosed by Hatchepsut at the very end. Barka can merely repeat her confession to him: « *– Je te quitte, à regret malgré le mal que tu m'as fait ... mais je te rappellerai un jour par delà les frontières de la vie* » (203). Eventually, two theories are offered for the rupture: the first, offered here, is that Kabar favored the suit of Thutmose III, Hatchepsut's rival, for her daughter's hand. The second, sexual jealousy on a more obvious level, is not offered until Hatchepsut's journals at the end.

In any event, the ultimate end to the birth/death imagery is a hope of resurrection or reincarnation. Thus, Barka evokes Biblical images of the lion lying down with the lamb, when the Middle East will find peace? In any case, there is an amalgam of Christian, Jewish and Islamic imagery. In Egyptology, the couple of Thot and Horus conceive and execute the Word: « Ces deux agents 'rendent effective la résurrection' » (205).

If the body is a temple, the Nile is its heart, its two ventricles being Luxor and Karnac. The body represents transcultural history, but also transtextuality. All the womb/tomb imagery prepares us for Barka's sudden death and the complete disappearance of his body, but not of his texts. It is Ibrahim who suggests he prostrate himelf before the statue of Hatchepsut, now complete, nose and all (207). According to Barka, « Les pierres invincibles m'entourent... » (206). He has an epiphany: « ... je reconnais l'instabilité et l'inconstance du savoir proposée à travers mes langues. Je sais que je ne connais rien et je reconnais ce que je sais » (207). He is in the passive state of mysticism, while Nisr is « sur le chemin des choix », crossing between Islam and Christianity – *il a le choix*. Barka is on a tightrope between past and present – he will soon make the choice, or the choice will be made for him.

The novel proper concludes with some exposition of the confusion (deliberately contrived) between the architect and his brother the scribe, who are alike as two drops of water. The presence of both brothers ensures that Senmut is omnipresent in the personal and professional life of Hatchepsut (210). That there are two brothers, moreover, reflects the doubleness of the text, as do the androgyny of Hatchepsut and the two crowns of Egypt. Barka finds his (Senmut the scribe's) real name, as he does « Ma langue substance du Nil » (211).

Barka draws an analogy between the love of peace and sexual love, both incarnated by Hatchepsut, and the « aïeux égyptiens qui ont sacrifié leur vie, en tous temps, pour une paix précaire à entretenir comme une amante capricieuse » (214). To recreate this past, « ... nous n'avons que des mots pour le faire » (214)[6]. Barka is a guilty lover, « pris en flagrant délit par mes propres mots » (215). Barka names the new form he creates a « narratoème », or a « Geste d'origines diverses » (215).

The tension between creation and fragmentation culminates here. Barka's being is destabilized, caught in a Baudelairean « forêt de symboles ». Barka affirms the joy of giving birth to words, « la seule activité essentielle de ma vie », just before dying. Historically, he is creating in the « Après

---

[6] As John Dos Passos once wrote, in the *U.S.A.* trilogy, "We have only words against ...".

Babel »[7]. He has travelled « dans les avalanches des langues », courting self-destruction. Is he suicidal, on the edge? He feels "decentered", and begins to wonder, in the name of Saint Augustine, whether it is indeed possible to resist the « Statue intérieure ».

Finally, the ground opens at the Hatchepsut statue and evidently swallows up the Barka we know. He feels a « mal au cœur atroce », then « un état second et me sens béni par les Dieux » (218). The ending is completely open, like the gaping cavern. Seeing himself as god of the underworld, the last words we have from him are: *« Je suis Horus, l'initiateur de ton œuvre à accomplir. Approche ... je t'offre mon Verbe ... regarde-le pulser ... dans sa vie éter...* ». In a similar stratagem to the story of Zitouna and Mansour, Barka's memoir could end, like Gide's *Journal des Faux-Monnayeurs*, « À continuer... ». Do words make the earth tremble? The trembling is also sexual, possibly signaling a final union with Hatchepsut.

Of Female Narratology

When Barka disappears, the women's voices take over[8]. Or rather, we realize that they have been in charge all along. The most important of the women is Francine Castel [Castle?], a world traveller herself. Despite her jealousy of Imane and Hatchepsut, she has the best of Barka, for she understands him completely, « le premier amour de sa vie qui le hante encore aujourd'hui » (49). Egypt was the dream of *their* youth, as it was that of Hatchepsut and Kabar. The first and last words of the novel are Francine's. Of the two prefatory remarks, seemingly from the dead Barka, the first consists of Francine's supposedly citing Barka, the second, the note "d. E.", is apparently also Francine's, for she is the editor, explaining the apparently disconnected, fragmented, sometimes lyrical, sometimes anecdotal form of the narrative. Ostensibly – and really – a carefully researched work, it follows the oral tradition of Orientalism; it is also stuffed with « notes, anecdotes », dreams, myths, and bits of information. But it is set in order by Francine, who is a Westerner and a female. And it

---

[7] The Tour CN will be the « Anti-Babel » in the novel to follow.

[8] Kenneth Fleurant notes that two female characters convey Bouraoui's themes: "Seeing the world as a mosaic helps us discover that contradiction and dissemblance are part of life and can be reconciled with the help of tolerance and justice. This is the lesson of humanists as old as Hatshepsut, as young as Imane" (1307).

is finally Francine who communicates (and interprets?) the words of Hatchepsut.

Margaret Lee is essentially a red herring, a stereotypical blonde Canadian tourist of sex as well as of foreign lands. Her brief affair with the frustrated Ayman is insignificant. Perhaps her primary function is to introduce her daughter Betty, the modern liberated woman, who will become Béchir's lover, but will also lead his father Rahmane back to a semblance of sanity – « c'est l'étrangère qui va ramener la brebis égarée au bercail » (199). Barka reminds us of the origins of Canada, resistant to revolution, with its echo of Hatchepsut's slogan: « Transformer la guerre en paix » (49). It is Francine who chooses Barka's hotel, the Hilwane, which is not luxurious, « mais tu auras le Nil à tes pieds » (50). Even her suicide attempt twenty-two years earlier seems to recognize Barka's fixation on death (86).

It is Francine as well who mentors Imane, advising her to study Senmut and the Maghrebian authors, rather than the Eurocentric Beauvoir and Duras. Her passion is described as "racinian"; she is a kind of Phèdre, as well as a passionate, suicidal Dido, Queen of Carthage. She knows she cannot do without Barka, but she criticizes his project acerbically. She mocks even his language: « ... celle que tu malmènes à la sauce Hatchepsout pour te faire un Nom dans la postérité... » ! (108).

She knows Barka as if she made him: « Je sais que ta capacité d'aimer est illimitée, comme d'ailleurs ta curiosité intellectuelle et ta voyance du marabout... Mais quand même ! Ma compréhension a des limites. Au fond, tu es comme l'eau du Nil... » (108). She constantly tries to anchor him to reality, and it is through her, the Frenchwoman and her French culture, that he discovers archaeology: « ... la France a mis au monde l'archéologie » (109). But she also warns him, « ... ne prends pas tes rêves pour de piètres réalités ». The resurrection of Hatchepsut may occur, « mais à quel prix ? » (110). Francine is the truth-teller: « Tu connais mon franc-parler ». She warns him not to bite off more than he can chew. Finally, Francine is unable to put together the fragmented body of her lover, but she is able to reconstitute his fragmented words.

Barka at times recognizes Francine's identification with Hatchepsut: « Je m'imprégnais progressivement de Hatchepsout à travers la chair de Francine » (134). Francine is also equated with Diana the Huntress, goddess of chastity, or Diane de Poitiers. Finally Francine, in an act of possession, refers to « son Barka », analogous to his possessiveness with Hatchepsut. In an important sense he is Francine's Barka, for it is entirely through her – well, partly through Imane – that we see him.

Ibrahim's part in all this is an insoluble mystery. Is he Senmut the architect, the killer of his own brother according to Hatchepsut's tablets? Is he hero or villain? He is the common man who first tells the tale of the woman who kills her husband, unveiling the dark elements of the dream. The Osiris story is also that of Cain and Abel, or fratricide. In what sense is Ibrahim Barka's brother? All this is related to the vegetation mysteries T. S. Eliot borrowed in *The Waste Land* from Jessie L. Weston's *From Ritual to Romance*. Isis presents the image of the ideal mother.

Ibrahim is a misogynist, warning Barka against women. Barka attributes his bias to class, lack of education, ambition and resentment – but is that all? As Barka says, « Mais jamais, je ne doutais de cet homme serviable » (200). Among other things, Ibrahim, like Béchir, is jealous of Ayman. Finally, it is he who suggests to Barka entering the forbidden zone, and, fatally, prostrating himself before the statue of Hatchepsut.

The Third Part begins with another female voice, in the form of Imane's letter to Francine which only partly fills the gap left at the end of Part Two. She gives the account of the only eye-witness, Ibrahim, who reports stones raining down on both their heads. « C'est un signe d'Allah », he says. Is it Judgment Day? An apocalyptic vision? Imane assumes that love equals knowledge (226). Thus, she affirms her beloved son Nisr, who is imbued with Barka's morality, as the dawn of the new social order. Imane recognizes without question that Barka's sole heir is Francine. She frames a bitter tale: « ... j'encadre à jamais le 'corrosif de sa narra-nativité' » (227). With respect to Barka's story, she is reporter rather than creator, though she creates in another sense, both biological and verbal, with her son.

Francine's three months of grief (mystic number) are one long, painful soliloquy: « Mon Barka m'a quittée à jamais ». She also establishes the parallel between the two women who seek to arrest Barka in time: « ... j'ai tenté de l'emmener avec moi dans le trépas mais sans succès. Hatchepsout, elle a réussi » (229). Barka's arrival in Egypt marks « le retour magnifié du scribe » who was Hatchepsut's lover.

Francine traces little by little the ties between the ancient Queen and the modern scholar.

Barka's « refus de religiosité dans ce monde » was less a rejection of religion than an affirmation of humanism emerging from cultural universality. Barka was nothing if not ecumenical. In her own time, Hatchepsut was a radical in religion, a monotheist before her time, and even before Akhnaton's: « Bien avant Akhénaton, la Pharaone était monothéiste, elle s'est réclamée descendant du Dieu Amon » (230). Like Barka, Hatchepsut was a humanist, integrating multiple diverse cultures: Hatchepsut « a créé les valeurs de la société 'occidentale', bien avant les Grecs et les Romains qui se prennent encore pour les premiers inventeurs de l'humanisme » (230).

For these reasons Francine and Barka share a common interest in Egyptology. Francine has confronted Barka with his apparent obsession with the unattainable, which makes him overlook the love close at hand: « ... notre amour est mort. Trop simple, trop terrestre n'est-ce pas ? Il te fallait pour le moins celui d'une princesse ? » (231). « Je l'ai trouvé », he replies, and admits, « ... même celui que j'ai ressenti pour toi n'en était qu'un pâle reflet ». He adds insultingly, « Toi, tu es trop charnelle » (232).

But in this penultimate section Francine comes into her own, transcends sexual jealousy, and arrives at a complex synthesis of ancient and modern, of love that overcomes the obstacle of time. Perhaps, in fact, she herself, by an act of imagination and love, becomes Hatchepsut:

> ... J'étais devenue déesse moi-même (peut-être plus encore que cette femme mythique sur laquelle les avis étaient si partagés), parce que j'avais réussi un tour de force, celui d'accepter qu'il soit enfin lui-même et non ce que je désirais qu'il soit. (232-3)

She shows a certain "heroinism" (to borrow Ellen Moers' term for the heroic in female protagonists): « Je saute quel que soit l'obstacle », though Barka does continue to live in her in his intimate objects still « tout imprégnés de son odeur » (233). She becomes a kind of detective, decoder, uncovering the clues and interpreting their language like a female Champollion.

She now begins to understand what he told her when they first met in a Humanities class at the Lycée Louis le Grand. He mentioned an earlier love, a first love, in the école, who had Oriental coloring: a little girl with black hair and charcoal eyes. At the same time, he had a crush on the teacher, who was blonde, like Francine, so Barka seems to have been torn between two passions all his life. If Francine works in Egypt, it is because it is the only way to destroy the ghostly object of her jealousy (233).

Imane, whose letter informs her of Barka's death, becomes a kind of partner: she passes on to Francine what they have found of Barka's writings. Francine, in turn, finds most of this narrative in his journal, or « cahier » (reminiscent of the « cahier de Meaulnes » in Alain-Fournier's *Le Grand Meaulnes*, subject of an earlier critical book by Bouraoui). Barka, or rather his writing, undergoes another reincarnation at the hands of Francine, who edits his text and notes to « faire bouger le cadavre de son roman ! » (235). In this she resembles the goddess Isis who brings her father back to life, and is kin to Hatchepsut. Francine is also an Ariadne finding her thread through « cette sorte de labyrinthe 'scriptural' » (234-5)[9]. Thus, in a spiritual and imaginative sense, she weds him at last.:

> Dans ce sens, Barka m'appartient depuis toujours. Ses écrits forment le contrat de notre mariage, nous unissant, par la création, au-delà des temps... Suis-je alors heureuse qu'il soit rendu à Hatchepsout par sa mort ? Fallait-il le sacrifier pour que fusion se fasse ? (235)

It is Francine who gives « un certain ordre » to this fragmentary manuscript, joining the bits and pieces into sections.

If Barka has been chosen as a kind of sacrificial goat, Francine wonders why Ibrahim, who has been sent to prison for three years for leading Barka into a forbidden, dangerous zone, killed him, if he did, and whether Hatchepsut inspired the crime in order to reclaim her scribe. None of this, however, explains the complete disappearance of the body.

Francine herself has found other writings in Barka's Samsonite case at the Hilwane, which turn out to be the « scriberies » of Hatchepsut herself. Ayman had found them in the hollow at the foot of the Sphinx, and had passed them on to Barka. These hieroglyphics are also left to Francine to decrypt. He kept his own writings separate from those of his muse or inspiration, hers in his right-hand pocket, his in the left (possibly signifying his illicit love).

Francine discovers yet another clue to the identification of Barka with the ancient scribe/lover of Hatchepsut: Barka always slept with the bedclothes wrapped around him like a turban, only his nose uncovered: « ... impression de coucher avec un revenant enturbanné qui ne me faisait l'amour qu'avec son *nez* ! » (237; emphasis mine). This habit of Barka's is linked with the missing nose from the Sphinx of Hatchepsut, but also with the scribe whose habit Hatchepsut mentions, « preuve irréfutable que Barka était bien l'incarnation du Scribe de la Reine ». Francine adds resentfully, but probably accurately, that Hatchepsut brought him back to earth, « mais elle n'a pas voulu me le laisser, à moi l'étrangère dont il était quand même amoureux, quoiqu'il en dise ! » (237).

Francine now embarks on her « projet d'en faire un livre » which will include Imane's letter, just as Barka recorded Francine's. Barka had even invented a pretended marriage with Francine whose details he recounted to a Nubian vendor (238), a sign of his vivid imagination. Francine

---

[9] Samia Harar compares Zitouna's guidance in the earlier novel to « le fil d'Ariane ».

reproduces some fragments, prose poems, written by Barka under the inspiration of a spectacular sunset on the Nile, a « Kaléidoscope vivant des inédits », from the « Nil des Mille et une Nuits », such as: *Les pêcheurs jettent d'immenses filets dans ce Nil en crépuscule. Je les vois tirer et retirer l'infini ... Labeur digne qui aura le dernier mot.* (239) The Nile is « *Un Au-delà qui est ici à nos pieds* » (239). The paradox of Barka's life, says Francine, was to lead us back in time in order to prepare the future. Did he poison himself with his own words? Francine doesn't think so.

We are left finally with a feminine narratology, Francine, Imane, and, with the last word, Hatchepsut herself: « Si j'ai donné à Imane la parole pour nous révéler sa version des faits, il me faut à présent déchiffrer les hiéroglyphes de la Reine et les mettre bout à bout... » (240). Francine concludes that she can only hold on to the reality of his writing. In *Retour à Thyna*, as well, it is the woman, Zitouna, who is left to complete the work of the dead Kateb by diffusing it throughout the country, and by adopting the male role of talespinner. She not only takes Barka's place, but becomes the voice of Hatchepsut herself: « Je lui prête ma main et mon âme pour me faire moi-même le nouveau scribe, en ce monde, de l'imbattable Déesse » (240). The ending does indeed suggest that history repeats itself, and that Francine does in fact, through a creative leap of faith, become Hatchepsut.

Hatchepsut's Narrative: The Voice of the Queen

In the end is the beginning. In a return to origins, the novel concludes, or rather comes full circle, with the « Journal intime » of Hatchepsut, in the form of « tablettes » inscribed with hieroglyphics which Francine has had transcribed, decoded, and translated into French. As Francine writes, « L'essentiel, c'est de donner la parole à la Reine. Peut-être le dernier mot de la fin qui est, en fin de compte, le commencement de l'histoire » (241). She also notes that Hatchepsut's style closely resembles the poetry of Barka, who may be the reincarnation of her lover/scribe. Does this mean the scribe influenced Hatchepsut's writing, or the other way around? The question is unanswerable because of the "silencing" of female writers throughout most of human history; thus « Hatchepsout écrivait en cachette sans se déclarer au jour comme 'scribe' elle-même » (241). So it seems that even queens and goddesses were silenced by a male hegemony. In any case, Hatchepsut wrote « poèmes en prose », anticipating Baudelaire – and Barka.

In the first tablet Hatchepsut suggests the Egyptian fascination with death, and a paradisiac after-life: « Je passe ma vie à bâtir le temple de ma mort » (242). Death is seen as a beginning, not an end – as is art. Hatchepsut introduces us to Senmut the architect and his brother Kabar, soon to be her scribe/lover, who also takes the name of Senmut when their love is consummated, to put the court off the scent. For the first time, as well, Pount, the modern African state of Somalia, is mentioned. A deliberate anachronism makes the Queen a foreseeing prophetess of the peace movement of the 1960s with the modern slogan, "Make love, not war" (242). Hatchepsut sees herself as the mother goddess Hator (possible source of her own name?): « J'allaite, Hator du Double pays, tous les enfants qui m'appartiennent ».

The second tablet introduces the theme of monotheism, confirming in her own words that the Queen is not only a political rebel, but also a religious iconoclast: « Il n'est de Dieu que Dieu » (242). And her God is Amun-Ra, the sun god, who was also later the Pharaoh Akhnaton's: « Moi, je me suis vouée à Amon, seul Dieu que je connaisse » (243). Her full name is "Khememet-Imen[10]-Hatchepsout", meaning « Lumineuse semence qui s'unit à Dieu » (243). She sees herself as « la protectrice de la perfection de Dieu », and denies the false rumor that she poisoned her father and her husband out of naked ambition to rule. Turning the tables on the men who accuse her, she says that it is their arrogance, their obsession with becoming God themselves, that lies behind all wars, a charge as relevant today as in ancient Egypt.

Tablet Three hints at the Queen's motivations in taking on some male attributes in order to assert her own vision of a world order steeped in peace and harmony. "Gender-bending", as we would call it today, becomes necessary to make credible any female empowerment. Hatchepsut is also coming very close to Virginia Woolf's definition of the "androgyny" that empowers the artist (in *A Room of One's Own*, 1929): « Changer de sexe... Mâle et femelle vivent en moi... Double vérité pour le Double pays ... nouveau né ... comme Rê ! » (244). The very structure of Bouraoui's text, in fact of most of his texts, is based on *dédoublement*, a doubling of characters who become alter egos, doppelgängers, even reincarnations of each other. This doubling is reinforced, in the fourth tablet, when she takes

[10] Is this the same stem as Imeni, Princess of Pount? And Imane?

the scribe as her lover, for Kabar « est l'autre moitié de mon être, celle que je garde dans mon *Kâ* ».

The fifth tablet concerns the fateful expedition to Pount, where the Queen is greeted warmly: « Bienvenue ô fille d'Amon, tu restaures tout ce qui est en ruines » (245). To the contrary of warlike [male] conquerors, she does not seek to impose « la surenchère des pouvoirs, dans leurs machines infernales [an echo of Jean Cocteau and the theater of « l'entre-deux guerres »] au nom de l'exclusif ! » (245). She is addressed as a fertile mother goddess, « Semeuse de lumière ! ».

The sixth tablet informs us that Hatchepsut has spent eleven years « de pure félicité » with her scribe (246). Three years before the end of her reign, she tells us, she decided to elevate him to the rank of Pharaoh by marrying him, although a commoner, but here sexual jealousy intervenes: « ... mais voilà que l'ingrat tombe amoureux d'une étrangère, la princesse de Pount qu'il a rencontrée en ma compagnie » (246). Could Hatchepsut have really raised a commoner to the status of Pharaoh? Were there any precedents? In any case, Hatchepsut herself introduces Girard's theme of "triangular desire », structural and thematic center of most of French, if not generally Western, literature. Certainly, Bouraoui's text is structured around the eternal triangle, of which the pyramid is the three-dimensional equivalent, where desire is inspired only by the presence of an obstacle, in the shape of a third party. The present-day triangles correspond strikingly to that of the ancient forerunners; thus we have Francine-Barka-Imane reflecting Hatchepsut-Kabar/Senmut-Imeni (princess of Pount). But also we have Ayman-Imane-Margaret Lee, and, crossing over the centuries, Francine-Barka-Hatchepsut – though it seems that Francine finally becomes Hatchepsut.

The sexual jealousy theme is, however, the one disturbing aspect of this novel. That Francine should be jealous of Hatchepsut is only natural and motivated – for how can one compete with a ghost, frozen in her perfection? But if we are to accept Hatchepsut as a truly liberated, generous, compassionate "modern" woman, it is difficult to view her also as not only jealous and vengeful, but capable of wanting to murder her rival, and of having her lover murdered, assassinated by his own brother – surely actions more characteristic of a warlike male Pharaoh like Ramses II.

The seventh tablet shows a Hatchepsut even jealous of her own daughter, whom she suspects of being at least infatuated with Kabar. Or does Hatchepsut see him as so desirable that no woman can resist him? At any rate, Hatchepsut arranges the marriage of her daughter to Thutmose

III. Hatchepsut finds herself in a cleft stick about Imeni, for she cannot expel her from her visit to Egypt without revealing her own illicit love for Kabar. But the previous tablet suggests that she was ready to reveal the secret anyhow, by making Kabar her consort (Pharaoh?).

Tablet Eight reveals a Hatchepsut seriously out of control, going mad from love and jealousy like any ordinary woman, and willing to sacrifice everything she has created – peace, prosperity, order – to avenge herself. She finds herself in the « Affres de la jalousie et de l'angoisse » (247). Now she feels that Imeni suspects her relationship with Kabar, who was formerly one with her, like the Word made Flesh. Hatchepsut soon lives the nightmare: « Je ne sais plus qui je suis ... ni ce que mon cœur désire... » (247). The statement echoes (prefigures?) Barka's own « décentrement » towards the end. At last she asks, negating everything we have been told about her as a radical force for good: « À quoi sert le pouvoir ? » (247).

The ninth tablet reveals the secret of the novel, which is to have its impact on the present-day lives of Barka, Ibrahim, Francine, Ayman and Imane. Hatchepsut confesses, « J'ordonne à Senmout de me venger », offering her heart and her crown to him in exchange for his brother's life – an old story of Seth, and, by implication, the Biblical Cain and Abel. She boasts, « Ma magie puissante triomphera de tous les obstacles » (248).

But by the tenth tablet she regrets Kabar's death, and we are invited to compare the deaths of Rahmane and Barka in the present tense of the novel. Kabar's body disappears, like those of both modern victims, and, like Rahmane's, it disappears into Mother Nile. It is also the story of Osiris repeated, torn to bits. Senmut the architect goes mad, and spends the rest of his life in « l'enfer de la folie » (248), for the brothers are alter egos. Hatchepsut forgets her supposed rival Imeni and is totally consumed by love. She wishes now only for death: « Je ne tarderai pas à rejoindre mon Kabar » (248).

Indeed, modern archaeologists have located a tomb thought to be Kabar's, and another reputed to be that of his royal mistress, the "Queen Who Would Be King", Hatchepsut. If they are correct, Hatchepsut ordered a tunnel to be dug between her tomb and her non-royal lover's, so that they might be together in the next world if not in this. Emily Dickinson's poem similarly invokes reunion with a dead lover: "I'd tunnel till my groove pushed sudden through to his...". The cave as a womb-tomb image is a familiar trope for the love-death theme, the « Nil'amourir » or « Amourir royal » theme which is central to the text.

In Tablet Eleven, Kabar speaks, as it were, from beyond the grave, for he has left a note on her pillow, explaining the apparent attraction to Imeni: « Jusqu'à ma mort, je ne saurais te trahir ! ... c'est pour nous protéger des mauvaises langues et du mauvais œil » (249).

In Tablet Twelve writing freezes life, and she imagines herself sleeping with him once more, his nose barely emerging from the bed covers: « Je revois encore son nez émerger de cette couverture naturelle ... Sans doute, aimait-il flairer dans son sommeil l'inspiration nécessaire à sa vie ? » The nose as an instrument of creativity? as a phallic symbol? Kabar had said, « Nous ne saurons jamais qui nous sommes jusqu'au moment où quelqu'un raconte notre histoire » (249). She had counted on him to be the taleteller of their « aventure exceptionnelle ». But we find in the tablets that she herself becomes the talespinner in his absence, as Francine is for Barka. At the same time, she sees him resisting imprisonment in his words: « Comment peut-il en être autrement, puisque l'écrit fige ce qu'il dit ? Voilà sa tragédie » (250). Life cannot be captured in so many words, but perhaps it can be shadowed forth in fragments and symbolically.

The thirteenth tablet (mystic number?) foresees Kabar's reincarnation as Barka Bousiris:

> Puisque j'en ai le pouvoir, je dois faire revenir Kabar sur terre, accepter de lui rendre sa liberté, et lui donner la possibilité d'assumer la tendre réconciliation qui nous unit, lui et moi, le monde et ses écrits ... J'ai mis entre nous des millénaires qui retarderont le moment de nos retrouvailles dans l'au-delà... Jusqu'à son retour à l'Origine, sa vie dans la modernité sera nourrie d'un destin qui lui restera inconnu et qu'il suivra avec d'autant plus de joie qu'il saura, cette fois, prendre pour amants le mystère de la force vitale et la liberté de la nommer à sa guise: envers de l'endroit qu'il façonnera et définira dans la sérénité de son *Ba*. (250)

"Ba" is defined in the Glossary as linking « les deux faces de l'être, le réel et l'imaginaire, le visible et l'invisible, le passé et l'avenir, la nuit et le jour » (253) – in other words, all the « doubles »of the novel, especially Bar/ka and Ka/bar – and it's all done with mirrors.

In Tablet Fourteen she recognizes that she will encounter her other half, « cette moitié de moi-même », only in « un monde sans limite » (250). She prophesies a perfect fusion in the distant future, « Un accédant du Tout céleste, je surgirai dans mon Unicité parfaite pour l'accueillir lorsque le temps sera venu » (250-1). We are invited to speculate whether it is Hatchepsut who caused the « tremblement de terre » felt by Barka just before his death. In that case, is the simple Ibrahim an unwitting reincarnation of the murderous brother Senmut?

The conclusion of the « Journal intime » of Hatchepsut is also the conclusion of the novel, and the last words consist of Hatchepsut's prophecy of Barka's achievements:

> Déjà la Paix me vient de ma certitude de son retour après qu'il ait semé l'espoir dans les cœurs endoloris, vidé les masques de leurs illusions, et rétabli la lumière dans l'univers de nos mains. (251)

Thus we end with a kind of envelope structure: a female editor (Francine, who admits that « j'ai opté pour un ordre arbitraire selon la façon dont je les ai trouvées dans le sac à dos de Barka » [241]), a female narrator (Hatchepsut), and a letter from Imane, all in praise of a *male* writer (Barka/Kabar) who seems to have passed the torch to the women. In the final analysis, all we know of Barka is his notes and research. Francine becomes more than a narrator/editor; she is the creative consciousness of the novel. In functioning as a creator, she accomplishes a similar gender crossover to Hatchepsut's. But she also arguably transcends her predecessor's achievements by overcoming, or mastering, sexual jealousy, destroying no one, but giving new life. Francine (aided by Imane) pieces the text together as if it were Barka's (or Kabar's) body. In so doing she surpasses, even replaces, Hatchepsut as female visionary. The novel on a whole, therefore, crosses genders and genres (lyric poetry, journal, narration filtered through multiple central consciousnesses), presenting a « double » vision, multicultural, multi-religious, multi-layered, abolishing time and space, and above all, androgynous.

roman

Hédi Bouraoui

Ainsi parle la Tour CN

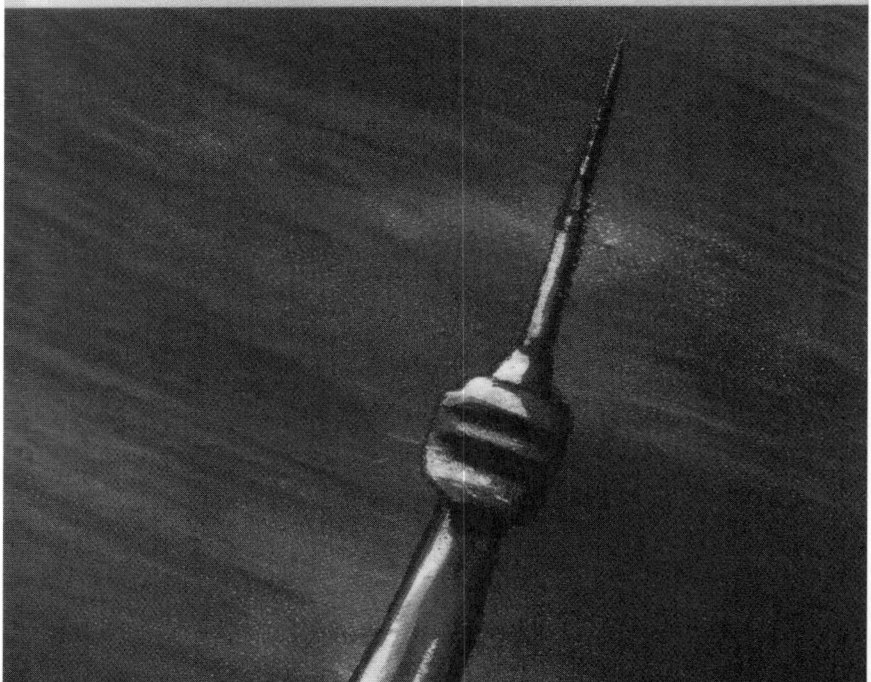

IV

Ainsi parle la Tour CN:

Of Moose and Women ... and Talking Towers

A Female Tower: « L'Anti-Babel »

Ainsi Parle la Tour CN (2000), Hédi Bouraoui's fourth novel,[1] like *Retour à Thyna* and, in a different sense, *La Pharaone* – in which the "exotic" suddenly becomes familiar, with an effect of « déjà vu » – represents a return to other roots. Here the return is to Hédi Bouraoui's longtime home in Toronto, Canada. The novel adds to his "literature of cities": Bangkok, Thyna/Sfax, Cairo, Toronto. Why the emphasis on cities? Because they are multicultural, diverse, and, at least in the case of Thyna/Sfax and Toronto, they are tolerant.

From the "stone lips"of the enigmatic Sphinx and the Pyramids we move to the concrete of the CN Tower, whose voice increasingly shifts in the course of the novel from « reportage », the « Babel » of modern telecommunications, to commitment, compassion, a « parti pris ». By the same token, the "phallic" tower of the opening, by taking a humanist stand,

---

[1] Pierre Léon calls it a « prosopopée » (8), but I prefer to think of it as a "lyric novel".

gradually adopts a female voice in keeping with the fact that, in French, « la Tour » is grammatically gendered feminine.

A finalist for the Trillium Award 2000, *Ainsi parle la Tour CN* is both timely and uncannily prophetic, as well as disturbing. It views the CN Tower as a powerful symbol for Toronto in particular, and Canada in general. Since the CN Tower, which is personified, competes with, and at the same time seeks a dialogue with, other towers around the world, Bouraoui also offers a vision of the Global Village heralded by Marshall McLuhan in the 1960s. The Tower transmogrifies into a human being (well, almost) in the course of the novel, in which it is the principal narrator. It embodies a kind of gender-crossover, gender-bending, so it is an androgynous tower. But the Tower becomes more human, sensitive, and committed as it explores its feminine side; I will therefore refer to it as "she" hereafter.

Is she our old friend, the omniscient author, the jovial Fielding presenting his "Bill of Fare" in *Tom Jones*, or the intrusive Thackeray, the puppet-master pulling the strings of his characters in *Vanity Fair?* Bouraoui, in fact, refers negatively to the latter: « Je ne joue pas au Bon Dieu qui tire les ficelles de ses poupées » (106). Like *Vanity Fair*, it is "A Novel Without a Hero", but it is definitely "A Novel with a Heroine", Twylla Blue, the abandoned wife of the Mohawk Pete Deloon, a woman of the First Nations, an Amerindian mystic, and a sculptor who works in stone. It is she who imbues the CN Tower with the true spirit of Canada – not the industrious beaver, but the mysterious, formidable, courageous moose of the Northern woods, « l'Esprit-Orignal »[2]. In fact, if you will, as in the previous novels, we have *two* heroines – Twylla Blue and the CN Tower, one made of stone (like the Sphinx) and the other human. At times, the two metamorphose spiritually into one. Twylla's name, in Arabic, means « long », associating her with the tallest tower in the world, as "Blue" evokes, among other things, *Bangkok Blues*. Twylla's global pilgrimage to the CN Tower's rival, the Menara Tower in Kuala Lumpur, Malaysia, confirms the echo of the Far East, and the circling of the globe.

The other characters are defined by their relationship with the Tower, as they come and go, hide in it, seek love or lust, leap off it, plot to blow it up. Of these, the most significant are Pete Deloon and his son by Twylla, Moki, Mohawk versions of Daedalus and Icarus (especially Joyce's), who

---

[2] Bouraoui introduced the moose in Canadian literature, giving it an important totemic, mystic role.

begin and end the novel, bringing it full circle; Souleyman Mokoko, the African engineer who operates the elevator until he is fired because of an unavoidable accident; Rocco Cacciapuoti, the ambitious Italian immigrant who becomes Minister of Communications – his responsibilities include the Tower whose principal purpose is to emit broadcast signals that cannot be blocked by the other downtown Toronto highrises (most notably the big banks) – but who yearns for his native Italy; Symphorien Lebreton, the frustrated would-be poet who conceals – or displays? – his writings in the Tower stairwells; and two secondary characters who provide comic relief – until the climax – Marc Durocher, the Québécois *de souche* and an activist for Québec separation (who beats his wife), and Marcel-Marie Duboucher, the Franco-Ontarian who feels compelled to join Marc's cause *faute de mieux* (who is gay).

Not long after the nominations for the Trillium Award were announced, the Toronto *Star*, purely coincidentally, on Saturday, April 1 – also the day of Pete Deloon's famous leap from the Tower – announced the intention of "the operators of the CN Tower" to extend its "height by at least 21.33 metres – all for the sake of the record books" (A1). The purpose is to retain Canadian "world class" superiority when the Kowloon MTR Tower is built by the Hong Kong government, which will reach a height of 574 metres (1,883 feet). The top of the CN Tower, its antenna, is 553 metres (1,815 feet). Pietre Von Jeste, speaking for the construction group hired to study the problem, says, "That 21 metres is our Everest. It's a peak we must surmount ... this thing is about a helluva lot more than just 68 feet" (A1). The Kowloon building will be both the tallest office building (rivaling Kuala Lumpur) and the tallest freestanding structure (rivaling the CN Tower) (A1, A22). Canada has three alternate plans: to "slice and stack" the Tower, slicing it just before the Sky Pod (where are you, Pete and Moki Deloon?), and then adding at least 66 concrete rings; or to use a "Pod Pump" to extend the Tower by 50 metres (possible problems with metal fatigue); or to replace the current antenna with a "sliding stick" that could be raised and lowered "much like an automobile radio antenna" (A1). The conclusion of the feasibility report confirms Bouraoui's view of Toronto: "A world-class city deserves a world-record building. And it's worth digging deep – to reach the sky" (I think Virgil said this first!) (A22).

On the same day, the *Star* published a "Letter of the Week", further supporting Bouraoui's view of the totemic value of the moose. The writer, Jane Champagne, responding to a March 17 piece in the *Star* entitled

"*Hogtown, Moosetown – 400 fibreglass moose to be city's newest attraction*", rebukes the *Star* for not naming "the artists involved in creating the multitude of moose destined to adorn Toronto streets". She then notes that "Charles Pachter [in illustration with moose picture] was the first Canadian artist to use the moose as a Canadian archetype in his paintings... One of his moose should have pride of place in Nathan Phillips Square..." (K7). Another artist sculpted a moose in Mayor Mel's image, CN Tower and all, and yet another "moose" appeared dressed as a Bay Street banker. Later, during the SARS scare, a pillow/mask was put over the muzzle of one of the remaining moose outside a hospital.

The Tower introduces herself arrogantly in the first sentence of the novel: « Tous les chemins mènent à moi et le ciel est ma limite », paraphrasing, "All roads lead to Rome", anticipating part of Rocco Cacciapuoti's function in the narrative, and "The sky's the limit". As the Roman Empire was, by definition, multicultural, so is Toronto, in the Indian meaning of its name, a « lieu de rencontres » (11). The Canadian debt to the First Nations is thus introduced from the very beginning, as is the Tower's even more immediate debt: « Mais qui au jour d'aujourd'hui est capable de chapeauter la plus majestueuse et la plus haute structure du monde ?... Seuls les Amérindiens ont pu me coiffer même si les hordes du monde m'ont fait surgir de ce sol qui leur appartient en première instance » (11). She stands beside Lake Ontario, and Pierre Léon reminds us that Bouraoui's lyricism is Whitmanian: it was, in fact, Whitman who celebrated "By Blue Ontario's Shore".

The Tower's movements are circular; her Revolving Restaurant turns 360 degrees in one hour, yielding views towards northern Ontario, to the South the United States, westward towards the Canadian prairies, eastward towards Québec, « la Belle Province ». There are distinct echoes of Georges Poulet's landmark text, *Les Métamorphoses du Cercle,* but perhaps more importantly in this context, of the mystic circle of the Indians, the circle of life. She herself says, « Je ressemble à cette Grande Roue du mysticisme indian. Cyclant l'Univers au cycle de la vie » (29-30).

The Tower is presented anthropomorphically. She becomes human by acquiring language. Initially, her language is transitory: « Je ne possède que la voix et l'image qui voyagent. Les nouvelles transitent en moi » (18). But she rebels against the ephemeral nature of her communication: « J'ai besoin de me détourner de ce flot incessant... Tout en évitant les longues tirades. Juste l'amour d'une ambiance créée dans le vertige des rêves. Pas celle d'un récit traditionnel » (18). The Tower always insists she is « anti-Babel » (where multiple languages were confused, with no one's understanding). And yet, she notes, one hundred fifty-seven languages are spoken in Toronto, but communication between linguistic groups is minimal. Like Nathaniel Hawthorne's Hester Prynne and Arthur Dimmesdale in *The Scarlet Letter* (1850), she yearns for the Biblical "gift of tongues", the Pentecostal tongues that descended on the disciples after Christ's death, speaking no known language, but understood by all[3]. In polyglot Toronto (and the world) the Tower is « la seule structure libérée du blindage des langues » (115). The Tower's first emission concludes, « J'anti-babélise. Ma voix intérieure susurre ses frémissements avant l'aurore » (18). Lest we miss the point that this is an anti-traditional tale (as an « anti-Babel »), there is on the opening page a hidden allusion to one of the fathers of the traditional novel, Balzac: « ... je suis venue parader ma splendeur et ma laideur », the reference being to Balzac's *Splendeurs et misères des courtisanes*[4]. Later she compares the suicide of Pete's cousin, a mere *fait divers* in modern journalism, to the treatment Balzac, Dickens, or Manzoni would have given it: two hundred pages for motive, two hundred for plan, two hundred for execution, two hundred for consequences (77). We are looking here at a « Comédie Humaine » for the millennium.

Parallel to, and contingent upon, her discovery of language is the Tower's discovery of history. Her creation in 1975 almost coincided with Pierre Elliott Trudeau's policy of multiculturalism. For the first time in history, a country encouraged immigrants to keep their own heritages. But they ended up being ghettoized, suffered high unemployment, exclusions of all sorts, so that the idealistic concept turned to vinegar (Bouraoui Interview April 24, 2000). As Bouraoui has said, « Je pose les problèmes du Canada actuel », and « Je ne condamne pas le passé » (Bouraoui Interview April 6, 2000). But one must understand it in order to create a dialogue

---

[3] Mohamed Chagraoui makes a similar point about the book's promotion of unity through diversity, though he does not specifically focus on the role of *linguistic* unity through diversity: « Dans *Ainsi parle la Tour CN*, l'universel repose sur la pluralité humaine ».

[4] Georges Bélanger remarks on the difficulty of the text, caused by the deliberate fragmentation: « Et, bien que *Ainsi parle la Tour CN* soit exigeant, difficile, parce qu'entre autres, il éclate le genre (le roman), qu'il se présente sous forme d'anecdotes fragmentées... » (32).

between and among cultures. Françoise Naudillon has remarked that « Le Canada est comme un laboratoire », but we have yet to see if the experiment is a success or a failure.

The Tower wittily describes her masculine origins, but it is important to remember that the genesis of the work – the building of the Tower – lay in the masculine aspirations of the power-brokers of Toronto – phallic ambitions that the Tower herself is to modify in the course of the novel:

> Tour Anglo-Saxonne, au féminin – ainsi me l'impose le français – , je me vois phallus géant, tendu, arc bandé aux pieds duquel on a eu le mauvais goût de placer un *Skydome* : vagin béant qui s'ouvre et se ferme à volonté. Sexe féminin, masculinisé par une grammaire que je ne maîtrise pas, juste pour l'amour de dénaturer nos rapports. Mais chacun tient à son sexe. (157)

The First Nations: The Delune Family

Pete De Loon: The Fall of Man

Pete's exploit begins the action of the book. He is Pierre Delune, "Moonstone" literally, and both stone – the stone of the Tower,[5] and the mystical stones of the Indians – play a major role in the narrative, as does the moon. Twylla Blue, his wife, resembles the moon, which is associated with the triple goddess of classical mythology: Diana the Huntress, goddess of chastity, who also presides over childbirth (the association with menses), and, later, the wise old woman – in fact, the three phases of a woman's life. The Tower prefers the crescent moon to the full moon, which leads us not only to the emblem of Islam, but all the way back to the Fertile Crescent of ancient times, the cradle of civilization: « Croissant fertile irrigué par le Tigre et l'Euphrate, Croissant Rouge, autre visage d'une Croix qui soigne ceux qui y croient » (87). Pete's name is anglicized into "Deloon", the loon of the lonely Northern lakes, another animal symbol, or totem, but also, as the

---

[5] Mohamed Chagraoui refers to the Tower as a philosopher's stone, « *la pierre philosophale qui les analyse avec l'objectivité du béton armé et la transparence du verre* » (16). But stone also evokes the Pyramids of the preceding novel. The referents are thus multicultural. Stone walls are also reminiscent of Melville's "Bartleby the Scrivener", subtitled "A Story of Wall Street", in which Bartleby the copyist refuses to copy, and beats his head against the dead blind wall. We learn at the end that he has worked as a clerk in the Dead Letter Office of the Post Office, which has driven him to despair.

"Loonie", symbolizing the cash nexus destroying him. Both « lune » and "loony" are associated with madness.

Pete in some ways encapsulates the language problematic posed by the Tower. As the Tower says, « Je suis de Souche et je suis fière de l'être !.. Au fait, je suis une Tour anglaise et je me narre en français. Ce n'est pas pour me vanter, mais j'aime prendre la parole de la minorité officielle » (21). Pete, like most Canadian Indians, has three names: an Indian, and those imposed by two colonizers, French and English – hence Pierre Delune becomes Pete Deloon. "Pierre" is also St. Peter, "Petros", the rock on which Christ founded his Church. Pete's mother, Naomi Crack, a white woman, who was not sure whether his *legal* father, or his cousin, was the biological father, abandons her son to the tender mercies of a convent school. Pete is thus trapped, biologically, culturally, religiously, and linguistically, between a white and an Indian world; between a totemic religion of nature, and an imposed Catholic faith; between French and English. His attraction to the two women, Twylla Blue and Kelly King, echoes this conflict. The Tower, by the same token, invents and speaks a "rocky language", « une langue rocaille », in her refusal to give in to the media waves passing through her. She is herself a futuristic variation on the totem pole.

Pete's leap from the Tower is, paradoxically, his high point in the novel, reminiscent of the leap of Robert Smith, the insurance man, from the roof of No Mercy Hospital at the beginning of Toni Morrison's *Song of Solomon* (1977)[6]. But Robert Smith's, haloed by Solomon/Superman/Sugarman imagery, is a leap of despair. Pete Deloon's is one of hope, albeit frustrated. But both Robert Smith and Pete Deloon are marginalized, a "black" man, who is one of Morrison's Seven Days (evoking the Black Panthers), and a "red" man. The former seeks either suicide, or a flight back to Africa – the scene is deeply ambiguous; the latter seeks to espouse modern technology in order to attract a white woman, with almost equally disastrous results. Both try to be Nietzschean supermen, but cannot even emulate the comic strip Superman. As well, Morrison's version of the flight back to Africa is that, if it is successful, the fathers leave their wives and children behind; if unsuccessful, it leads to self-destruction. Pete has left his wife and child behind, and risks self-destruction, one way or another.

---

[6] Moreover, there is an important "Solomon" figure in Bouraoui's novel, who also happens to be black: Souleyman Mokoko.

The reader is initially inclined to see Pete as the hero, but that role will pass eventually to his son Moki, who repeats, in a different vein, his father's exploit at the end of the novel, as it, like the Tower, comes full circle. In fact, Pete's leap constitutes a paradigm of the Fall of Man. It takes place, appropriately, on April 1, Poisson d'Avril in French, April Fool's Day in English. If so, Twylla Blue is a kind of new Eve, who loses her innocence through her husband's abandonment of her and his fall; but she is also a Madonna for the modern age, left with a son, Moki, a kind of new Christ, with no real father to speak of (like little Pearl in *The Scarlet Letter*) except his Heavenly Father. She is also a faithful Penelope to her far-wandering Odysseus, Pete: « Pénélope abandonnée dans la réserve, elle attend en vain le retour d'Ulysse ! » (123). It is Pete who enables the Tower to "speak", « ce premier jour du mois farceur », and Bouraoui comments wryly, « Parler et déparler, c'est la valeur vitale du pays » ["To speak or not to speak, that is the question ! »]

Far from being self-destructive (at least intentionally so), Pete's leap is in aid of life, albeit to impress a fantasy "dream girl", the Beautiful Blonde, Kelly, who directs the daily running of the Tower from her office, seated in front of a small television screen. For the Mohawk, as for the black male, the white woman might as well be wearing a sign, "Look, but don't touch"[7]. In a lovely image, we are told, « ... il rêve d'elle. Il déguste son sourire comme une orange de Floride » (16). She is as unattainable as a dream, as distant as Florida – and he is ignoring the happiness in his own backyard – Twylla.

Pete tries to use his "Indian" gifts – a head for heights, a ceremonial dance – to attract Kelly's attention. He is drawn by the « vue plongeante » (16), but also by the Beautiful Blonde, who hasn't even smiled at him on the day of his great exploit:

> Le Contremaître hurle : *For God's sake Pete don't screw up this job!* À ce moment, il lui prend l'envie de danser sur le petit carré à la racine des quatre branches de l'antenne. Danse traditionnelle de Mohawk que son ami ne peut s'empêcher de photographier pour la postérité. Encouragé

---

[7] Eldridge Cleaver, in *Soul on Ice*, refers to the white woman as "the Ogre" for this reason, and Ralph Ellison, in *Invisible Man*, shows the white men at the smoker using a naked blonde white girl with an American flag painted on her belly being used as an instrument of control over the young black men who are present supposedly to receive college scholarships.

> par cette prise folle en image, il endosse un parachute et plonge dans ce laps de temps de l'année miracle 1975. Cascade tellement osée qu'elle surprend les amis, les travailleurs, les passants... (17-18)

Except for the Beautiful Blonde who is relieving herself in the basement washroom, instead of observing Pete's flight on her closed circuit TV screen.

From this moment on, the Tower begins to take the side of her characters: « Comment puis-je agir en sa faveur ? Moi Tour CN » (18). She adds, moreover, "I am what I tell" (97). She knows that life can't be learned, but is determined to study it nevertheless. Her wording, also, suggests that *Ainsi Parle la Tour CN* is in the great tradition of Canadian apprenticeship novels, but in this case the « apprentice » is a Tower, not a young man! Pete's Adamic fall from innocence is echoed by the Tower's, and she identifies her powerlessness to help specifically with the limits of her media-ted language. The Group of Seven, she comments, have described the Canadian landscape better than she can (89). From the time of his fall, Pete begins to deteriorate, turning increasingly to alcohol and drugs, the white man's curses imparted to the Indians, with their congenital vulnerability. He is skeptical about the whole issue of language between Québécois and Anglophones, compared to the Indians' plight (even while recognizing that it was worse, in terms of violence, in the U.S.). Language quarrels, according to him, pale beside the genocide of the Indians on the other side of the border, their de-culturation, the "planting out" of their children, the sexual abuse of children in the name of progress and the 1842 law confining the Indians to reservations, the systematic theft of their land by these so-called "founding peoples! Forget it!" (35).

We are not privileged (if that is the right word!) to witness the start of his relationship with the hitherto aloof, indifferent Kelly. Perhaps it doesn't really interest the Tower, who is not very happy with Kelly at her controls, and who comes to adore – perhaps identify with – Twylla: « Je ne vous ai pas raconté comment Kelly s'est laissée charmer par Pete » (155). If the Tower is « sans pensée », Kelly « pense mais n'existe pas » (155). The novel tends towards a complete repudiation of Cartesianism – « Je pense, donc je suis » – and a strong affirmation of existentialism – « Existence precedes essence » – which is totally alien to the computer- and law-programmed Kelly.

Pete's disillusionment is not long in coming: « Pete a l'impression de serrer des algues sèches au lieu de la sirène de la nuit, sortie des gouffres de l'enchantement» (156). As the Tower comments sardonically about Kelly's hypocrisy, « Le saut dans le lit de Kelly était une aventure d'amour en dents de scie » (236), while Twylla is « sa libératrice d'antan et d'aujourd'hui; moi aussi [adds the Tower] ». Kelly, with her sexual coldness and manipulativeness, is, in fact, all too representative of "traditional" Canada, whose long winter covering of snow makes her distinctly resemble a whited sepulchre, this country of non-belligerence and neutrality, with its « réputation de blancheur immaculée » (50). In front of the Henry Moore statue in Nathan Phillips Square, Pete himself is moved to become an oral talespinner, when inhabited by the Moose-Spirit: *« J'ai fait l'amour à deux femmes aussi différentes que le soleil et la lune » (233).* Twylla, the moon spirit (or goddess?) is his own true love, which he recognizes too late, for she has found her soulmate Zinal.

Twylla reads mystic blue and turquoise *stones*, echoing her husband's first name, as well as her own last name (233-34), and Moki, their son, appears in Pete's vision carrying an emerald stone, *« transformée en pierre de clarté »* (235; emphasis mine). The family reenacts the Indian circle of life: « *Je me dirige vers l'est, je trace un cercle par terre, et je place les sept pierres du nord à l'est, puis du nord à l'ouest, trois de chaque côté* » (235). The Tower, herself a stone construction, also turns 360 degrees in one hour. The Moose-Spirit (« Esprit-Orignal » in French) is also the « Esprit-Originel », a return to origins. The Amerindians and recent immigrants empathize in their faith, as in so many other ways: « *Nous, Amérindiens et immigrés récents, nous en faisons notre foi qui est ancrée au Créant* » (235).

Except for his vision at the end, Pete virtually disappears from the text after his heroic/foolhardy leap. He is mired in an ill-fated affair with Kelly, which is described as « un nœud de vipères » (55) – another literary reference, this time to François Mauriac. Kelly is perhaps the least successfully realized character in the novel, as she is somewhat stereotypical. She has an Electra complex, but has been unable to express her love to her father. Her mother dies thirsting for love, and Bouraoui describes the « Froideur d'un père qui porte un masque voilant toutes les douleurs » (46). She is "tolerant" of Marcel-Marie's homosexuality – « L'homosexualité ne la gène pas » – which she understands not as an active sex drive, but as « un besoin intérieur de s'enfermer en soi », a need she herself feels. In a nice phrase, we are told she is « murée en elle-même comme une citrouille autour de ses graines, elle ne peut exprimer ses sentiments à personne » (75). Not surprisingly, the one confidante she finds is another woman, Suzy

McNally, with whom she has a lesbian affair, but the sexuality is subordinate to the repressions of both women. Somehow it is hard to believe that she would have the sensitivity to quote William Blake: "To see the world in a grain of sand/And heaven in a wild flower" (102).

Twylla Blue: « L'Esprit-Orignal » and the Spirit of the Tower

Twylla Blue is the true heroine of the novel, as opposite to Kelly as the moon is to the sun. In most mythologies, the sun is masculine (Apollo), while a female principle presides over the moon (Diana). Twylla introduces Pete to Protestantism in Saint Paul's Chapel at Brantford: « Dans cette chapelle Mohawk, bâtie en 1785, son épouse Twylla Blue, protestante, l'avait amené pour qu'il lui jure fidélité dans une religion qui n'est pas la sienne » (80). More importantly, however, she embodies the spirit of Amerindian religion, which encompasses all religions in harmony with nature, as in the prayer, « *Et vous, oh Jour/Et vous oh Nuit !/Tous vous me voyez/en unisson avec ce monde* » (80).

Twylla's spiritual ancestor is the famous Mohawk pœt, Emily Pauline Johnson: « Cette fille célèbre du Chef Mohawk, née à *Chiefwood*, a voyagé à travers le monde, comme poète et actrice, pour expliquer le tort que les Blancs ont infligé à son peuple. Elle a entrepris sa mission avec une passion et un zèle jamais égalés jusqu'à présent » (81). Twylla, like Pauline Johnson, adventures to other worlds, as far as the Menara Tower in Kuala Lumpur, Malaysia, where she encounters Zinal, who will become the love of her life. Zinal seeks refugee status because he has aided his mother, as she had wanted, to die mercifully. Twylla and Zinal strongly resemble two characters in the earlier *Retour à Thyna*, Zitouna who tries to liberate herself in order to liberate other women, and the shy journalist Mansour, whom she chooses for an egalitarian marriage. While Pete leaves Twylla, with their child Moki, on the reserve with its hospitable motto, « Venez vous joindre à nous ! », she not only follows him to the city, but repeats, and extends, Pauline Johnson's world travels.

The Tower cannot save the marriage, any more than she can save Pete's job: « Trait d'union entre ciel et terre, je n'ai pu reconcilier Pete et Twylla » (123). She is neither omniscient nor omnipotent. But she presents Twylla as a true heroine, who is faithful to Pete « malgré la tradition qui lui donne tant de liberté » (123). Like Zitouna, Twylla is both modest and a life force. The Tower compares her to a powerful sea (whose tides are controlled by the moon): « Si elle s'efface par modestie, c'est qu'elle s'affirme pour rendre à la vie toute sa saveur. Twylla possède le charme et l'art de vous attirer à elle comme la mer aux fleuves vagabonds » (123). She has no need of technology (unlike Kelly) to find her way in Toronto: « Internet sans ordinateur ! » (125). As the Tower seeks to find her identity through language, Twylla finds her vocation as a journalist (like Mansour), going to Rocco Cacciapuoti to seek a position. Twylla thinks, evoking a central image of *La Pharaone*, the female Pharaoh being another powerful woman, Hatchepsut: « Il faut s'adresser au sommet de la pyramide, si on veut la grimper. Jamais aux intermédiaires, ni à la base » (126). The Tower herself is also a kind of elongated pyramid. She realizes that Twylla, like herself, is in quest of language: she is going to « partir à la conquête du nouveau langage des tours pour faire trôner ma réputation auprès des grandes audiences du monde entier » (126).

If Twylla Blue espouses the cause of the Tower, the converse is also true – the Tower finds a kindred soul in Twylla, a kind of sisterhood: « Toutes les deux, nous serons constamment l'une en face de l'autre, même si elle côtoie la Mer de Chine du Sud et moi, le bord du Lac Ontario » (129). In Malaysia, Twylla proves to be typically Canadian in aiding Zinal to emigrate to Canada: « Comme tant de bons Canadiens, elle pense aider le autres avant les siens ! » (142). By the same token, Twylla finds her mate in Zinal, whose name means literally « le Beau », the Handsome One. They even look alike, « ce couple à la peau brune, aux yeux bridés, au visage eurasien... » (140). Malaysia, like Canada (Toronto in particular), like Tunisia, is a crossroads of cultures, a « plaque tournante ». The Kuala Lumpur Tower is a "Menara" or "Menora": « Le premier mot en arabe veut dire phare, le deuxième en hébreu, bougeoir à sept branches. Celle du milieu sert à allumer les trois de chaque côté » (145). But what matters is that both words, for both cultures and religions, signify light. Zinal offers Twylla balm for her wound, the same gift Zitouna, whose name signifies olive, including olive oil – used for healing, light, and food – offers Mansour.

On her return to Toronto, Twylla has a dream in which her own voice and that of the CN Tower seem to mingle, merge: « *Je ne suis ni rétrograde, ni un Zarathoustra qui persiste à vouloir enseigner le surhumain. Je n'ai de leçon à donner à personne* » (147). Twylla does not want to be the Nietzschean superman (or superwoman), evoked by Pete in his leap from the Tower, but rather to substitute the Moose-Spirit, « l'Esprit-Orignal », for the superhuman. And the « Esprit-Orignal » is the spirit of a natural language stretched to its limits, not of a supernatural. The Tower comments on Twylla's "sisterhood", which gives the latter « la parole rocaille » and lifts her burden as a mute witness (147).

At the May Pow-wow at Sky Dome, Twylla falls into a trance and uses her prophetic voice to see the past clearly and foresee the future. Different in appearance, at birth, from the other members of the tribe, they named her "Twylla" because she had "blue-grey eyes" (169), and seems therefore of mixed heritage like her husband Pete. As a baby, she sleeps and eats "like a stone", again a prophecy of her marriage to Pierre Delune. Her eyes are turquoise, a magical color to the Amerindians since it represents both sea and sky, like the turquoise stones: « *Ces pierres à la forme brute sont de grosses pépites turquoises ramassées de la Terre Mère ... à un moment donné une de ces générations saurait s'en servir pour aider la tribu* » (173). Twylla is thus linked to the Magna Mater, Earth Mother.

Twylla also expresses herself in writing, drafting a report to Rocco Cacciapuoti, this « petit Napoléon ». She pays the Tower the tremendous compliment of seeing its disinterestedness in the midst of the Big Banks (175). As the Tower herself has said, « ... les gratte-ciel ... ont l'air de faire des courbettes à mes pieds » (38). Twylla notes, however, that the Kuala Lumpur Tower is metaphysical as well as physical, incorporating « arabesque » forms, as the Koran dictates, which do not spring out of nature, and offering every visitor a "*SALAMAT DATANG*", or « *Salut de la Paix* » (177):

> *Leur Tour possède donc un vernis mystique puisque* The whole tower head is clad in glass ... arranged in the traditional islamic form of the « MUQARNAS ». *Toute la structure devient alors une entité harmonieuse reflétant la renaissance de l'héritage architectural islamique. La Tour de Kuala Lumpur est dotée d'un Esprit que, malheureusement, la nôtre ne possède pas, et ne semble pas vouloir posséder.* (177)

These designs are reminiscent of the ancient mosaics in *Retour à Thyna*. The CN Tower is not yet ready to receive the Moose-Spirit: « *Personnellement, je sens l'Esprit-Orignal rôder autour de la tour au lieu d'en émaner, comme des prières de cœurs incrédules* » (178).

Twylla's Asian experiences have enabled her to transcend her unhappiness at Pete's infidelity: « *... je ne compte pas arracher Pete aux griffes de Kelly* » (175). She sues him for divorce only to support their son Moki, and she even retains a grain of sympathy for the naïve, victimized Pete, who has allowed himself to be coopted by the system, represented by Kelly: Pete is a fly caught in Kelly's spider-web (or Venus flytrap?), and, moreover, she does not help him find work or insurance, keeping him dependent on her like a pet dog.

The animal imagery springing up in Twylla's thought-processes is far from the totemic powers associated with the moose and other animals sacred to the Indians; it evokes, rather, animal appetites. If the Tower is a giant totem pole, the animal imagery is also cross-cultural, for the tale is told « à la manière de La Fontaine avec ses animaux » (99).

Twylla appeals to Rocco's somewhat similar Mediterranean « indulgence » to give her free-lance work as a journalist. She shows her sense of humor, as well as her awareness of what the First Nations and the newest immigrants have in common: « *Cela me permettra de mettre un peu de graisse de caribou dans mes spaghettis* » (178). Rocco is far less willing than Twylla, however, to acknowledge the attractions of the CN Tower, since he remains firmly rooted in his native soil – in fact, can't wait to return to it. He asks why

> *... la verticalité de la Tour CN me laisse froid comme un stalagmite en mal de pesanteur ? Œuvre gigantesque à l'époque, cette tour de ma terre natale est aujourd'hui une naine qui n'atteint même pas un dixième de la Tour CN.*
>
> ...
>
> *Debout et rectiligne notre Tour CN provoque le monde par sa rectitude. Et je comprends mieux maintenant l'intention de Twylla d'insuffler à cette farouche partisane de laïcité l'esprit-orignal ! Elle ne penche pas comme la tour de Pise.* (221)

In Tour 16 Bouraoui (the Tower?) describes Twylla's magical encounter with the Esprit-Orignal. "Hunting", like a modern Diana, armed only with a camera in the northern Ontario woods, « elle cherche à saisir l'instinct divin et immortalise l'orignal » (211). Encountering him standing in the water, Twylla focuses and snaps her picture: « L'orignal pose, laisse montrer ses atours et lui jette un regard admiratif. Elle a osé l'affronter » (212). Her admiration, and Bouraoui's/the Tower's are evoked by the multiplicity of this symbol, representing a nation of multiplicity. Thus, it embodies all the natural colors of Ontario, as well as a number of different animals representative of different cultures making up the Canadian mosaic:

> Est-il de la famille du daim avec ses bois aplatis ? De celle du chameau avec sa bosse sur le dos ? De celle du cerf avec ses pattes fines ? De celle du cheval avec son mufle dilaté et élégant ?... Mais ce qui l'étonne

> le plus, c'est que son poil est mêlé de gris, de brun, de rouge et de noir ... de tonalités qui s'harmonisent avec la couleur du terroir ! (212)[8]

Twylla (and the Tower) admire most of all the fact that the moose, like Canada itself, is « maître de sa destinée : Contrairement au cerf qui s'affole et suit le cours du troupeau, l'orignal suit sa nudité virtuose » (212). The moose also appeared traditionally on the Canadian quarter, like the loon on the dollar. But Twylla, like the Tower, rises above material concerns, in favor of the love of the land. The Tower describes Twylla's experience in the northern woods as a « Digne rencontre de la fille de la Première Nation avec l'animal qui l'accueille dans son sein. Maîtrisé. Cette symbiose retenue est devenue rituel de recueillement » (213).

It is Twylla who introduces this Esprit-Orignal to the Tower, giving the latter equal spiritual status to the Menara Tower in Kuala Lumpur:

> Twylla dont le visage de pleine lune[9] trahit maintenant une joie fulgurante, emporte l'orignal, à bras le corps, en mon sein... Sans tarder, l'animal se marie à ma chair de pierre, et fait de moi une ville *prévoyante* et non « flamboyante » comme d'autres Capitales. (213)

In effect, the *masculine* Esprit-Orignal impregnates the female Tower of stone, turning stone into living flesh like a Pygmalion animating his statue of Galatea. From this point on the Tower seems increasingly to think of the characters passing through her as her children, her offspring. Thus the maternal Twylla transforms the Tower into a symbol of maternity. It is the Tower who, « grâce à Twylla », explores the meanings of the Esprit-Orignal, and ties them to her discovery of a language that accommodates all cultures and religions:

> *... j'ai appris à lire l'esprit-orignal qui, se situant dans l'entre-langue, prône la séparation entre le temporel et le spirituel au lieu de celle du Québec avec le reste du Canada. Symbiose des religions et des cultes, l'esprit-orignal s'accommode de différences parce qu'il est tolérance...* (217)

---

[8] Georges Bélanger describes the « Esprit-Orignal » as « ... l'esprit rassembleur, aux multiples facettes : elle représente à la fois la force de la terre, la nature, la liberté, l'amour, la pureté, la tolérance, et seul gage de l'avènement d'un monde nouveau... » (32).

[9] By this association she surmounts symbolically even the Tower itself, as well as reminding us that she has been the wife of Pierre De Lune.

Until this vision the Tower cannot speak truly: « ... il m'est difficile de démonter les êtres, d'exprimer leurs ressorts complexes avec les mots alors que je ne suis qu'une tour de pierres et de ciment... » (156). Is it the Esprit-Orignal that endows her with the gift of speech?: « Irai-je jusqu'à dire que c'est l'Esprit-Orignal qui parle à travers moi ? » (160).

Moki: The New Utopia

The third member of the De Lune family, Moki, like Nisr in *La Pharaone*, can be seen as a kind of savior. He brings the seven stones (seven days?) buried in the Tower's innards to his mother. Twylla chooses three, shaped like a bear, representing world leadership, a wolf, representing light and energy, and a tortoise, representing wisdom and the natural order (237-38). Twylla is to make her career as a sculptress of soapstone animals. Twylla dreams again of the « Voyant-voyageur » with pale grey-blue eyes (herself and her son) who appears in each generation (239). The Tower's "trances", even, echo Twylla's (161).

Moki is to repeat his father's exploit, but in the opposite direction; he *climbs* the Tower, like Spiderman, rather than leaping off it, and ascent also implies descent, but no Fall of Man. The Tower describes the circular adventures of De Lune père et fils:

> ... Il [Moki] palpe la pierre qui pend à son cou et s'aperçoit qu'elle a pris ma propre forme de Tour CN en miniature. L'Élan des Airs souffle en lui l'haleine de l'arc-en-ciel, dilate son corps et son esprit et lui arme les pieds de ventouses. À la stupéfaction de tout le monde, Moki se met à m'escalader. Il grimpe comme une araignée, à mains nues. Comme son père, il veut, en solo, vaincre temps et pesanteur... Perché à l'endroit même d'où son père avait sauté, Moki fut envahi par une extrême sensation de jouissance. Maintenant il sait qu'il peut, à son tour, retourner vers la terre. (272)

« Jouissance » is the word Roland Barthes used to evoke « *Le Plaisir du Texte* », (1972), and we are once again reminded that this is a book about language. Lest we forget, Moki wants to replace the advertisement for "Microsoft Windows 98 Start" by his own banner, « À livre ouvert/Troisième millénaire » (272). The young Moki seeks to « rendre justice à son père qui fut le premier à défier le gouffre du vide » (276). Not only does the flight metaphor associated with both father and son make them clearly analogous to Joyce's version of the Daedalus and Icarus legend, it also suggests that they are would-be artists. Moki's adventure is a poem: « L'exploit de Moki est un cri flottant dans le bleu du vent qui laissera sur le parchemin du temps l'ancrage d'un poème d'amour filial » (276). The Tower tries hard to tell his story: if language reflects the soul of a people, why can the stones not also « exprimer l'Esprit-Orignal de ce Moki prédestiné à extirper du Ciel une lumière inédite ? » (277).

From here Moki returns to the tribe and tries to put into practice a Utopian and natural (small-c communistic) ideal. For this, as for his anonymous exploit, he receives no more thanks from Toronto than his father before him. The RCMP investigate him and consider him guilty of "revolutionary ideas": « Moki est arrêté le jour de mon anniversaire, le 26 juin, pour atteinte à la sécurité de l'État » (281). Moreover, he is jailed without a trial for showing tourists areas of the reservation they were never supposed to see (282). In fact, he tried to keep a certain Mr. Smith, a tourist, from invading his garden, and a disturbance ensued. The police inspector who questions him, himself a recent immigrant from Mauritius, becomes, reluctantly, fascinated by Moki's project, including the teaching of the Indian circle of life, analogous to the 360-degree turn ("revolution" in another of its meanings) of the Tower: « ... nous apprenons à nos enfants à penser le temps comme nos ancêtres, autrement dit : en cercle et non pas en ligne droite. La linéarité occidentale est révolue et nous ne cultivons pas les carottes et les navets en rangs d'oignons, mais en circularité donnant à la ligne droite une flexibilité qui lui permet de se mouvoir sur 360 degrés » (286). He is as hard on the Cartesian notion of creating a universal language as the Tower, and Bouraoui, are on the Cartesian "cogito", seen earlier in relation to Kelly.

Once released from prison, Moki carries his "revolution" to the Queen City, where his mother now lives with Zinal and sculpts stone: we are reminded of Henry Moore's dictum that the ideal statue pre-exists, embedded in the stone, needing only to be liberated by the sculptor. Twylla urges her son to rebuild our country to match the height of the Tower. Love, the creator, is guided by « l'écume des jours »,[10] lifting the Moose-Spirit to the top of the Tower (288). Twilight prepares the dawn, she says.

The "mothers" seem to be the characters who prepare for the new day: we have not only Twylla and Moki, but Madame Lebreton and Sympho-

---

[10] This is another literary allusion, to Boris Vian's novel.

rien, whose central concern is language, and the Tower herself. The Tower has more affinities with the Statue of Liberty in New York Harbor than with the Empire State Building. The latter has nothing feminine or "female" about it; it is a purely phallic symbol[11]. The Statue of Liberty, on the other hand, is maternal; it looms protectively, like a Tower, over New York, the financial district in one direction, the open sea in the other. She is pyramidal in shape, like the CN Tower, leading to the peak, the summit, the Torch of Liberty. She is bicultural, presumably bilingual, a gift from the French Government; indeed, a small Statue of Liberty still rests on an island in Paris. Moreover, she can speak; in the words of Emma Lazarus:

> Give me your tired, your poor,
> Your huddled masses yearning to be free,
> The wretched refuse of your teeming shore,
> Give, please, the homeless, tempest-tossed to me;
> I lift my lamp beside the golden door.

Like the CN Tower, one can climb inside her for the view, a "penetration" with sexual implications. And both Lady Liberty and the CN Tower are defenders of the powerless, the new immigrants, but only the Canadian Tower sees herself as equally a defender of the First Nations. Twylla, at the end, leads a delegation of the First Nations supported by the complete spectrum of the masses of recent immigrants who, despite quarrels and misunderstandings, have succeeded in living together in tolerance (334).

Two Female Voices: From « Dialogue de Sourds » to Communion?

Kelly King, however, has nothing of the maternal about her. In fact, when she was very young she abandoned her baby on the church steps, and is now being unfaithful to Pete with her confidante, Suzy McNally, while Pete descends further into alcohol and drugs. At the very end of the novel there is a dialogue established between Twylla and Kelly. Bouraoui does stack the cards, because Twylla mentors Kelly. The latter's name combines Irish-Celtic (Kelly) with Anglo-Saxon (King). She is at the controls of the Tower, but knows nothing of its working – a little like the white men who think they operate the Paint Factory in Ralph Ellison's *Invisible Man* (1953),

---

[11] The novel was written and published before the horrific destruction of those other phallic symbols in New York, the twin towers of the World Trade Center.

while it is a black man, Lucius Brockway, who is really in control, in the basement, and who has invented the process producing white paint with black "dope". Kelly has abandoned herself totally to the « capitalisme - régnant », and has slipped up only with Pete (341). She deals in stereotypes about the Indians: that they lack the spirit of enterprise, that they are rooted in magic and mysticism, that they want to transform the Tower into a teepee or igloo (341-2). Twylla paraphrases a French proverb to this representative of "Anglomania": « Oui, je vous vois venir avec vos grosses Adidas ! » [« avec vos gros sabots » in French, said of French peasants].

Twylla denies adamantly that she is « une passéiste ». Neither is the Tower, a product of the postmodern age, and therefore technologically sophisticated. But the Tower does say that « Le passé ne me hante pas, le présent j'essaie de le résoudre... », but that « L'avenir m'effraie » (136). Moki, too, knows computers, but seeks to humanize them. Twylla warns Kelly to "pay attention"; this is a reference to the final line of Arthur Miller's *Death of a Salesman*– "Attention must be paid", says Linda Loman of her husband Willy, at the same time an accomplice and a victim of the capitalist mentality. Kelly is commanded to pay attention to the saying: "Don't judge others if you have not walked in their moccasins" (342).

Kelly admits that « nous n'avons pas assez formé d'autochtones en matière d'éducation, gestion ou politique » (341-2), but what she is really describing is a process of assimilation, loss of identity. Kelly allows that the majority culture has pursued material progress at any price, and Twylla cautions that the rampant spirit of enterprise has lost all spirituality, though lip service is paid to it. She knows that one cannot pour new wine into old bottles, and that the world of the future must be created peacefully: "We will not conquer with *iron*, unlike you, but with *stone*", the stone capturing the cadence of artistic inspiration (343-44). The Indians must surmount their anger, the whites their guilt over persecuting the Indians.

The novel ends in an apocalyptic vision. Twylla sees them « au point de non-retour, à l'avant-dernière heure de l'Apocalypse » (344). She foresees the restructuring of the Province, the country ... and finally the world (342). Salvation, she affirms, will lie in "tour-ne-soling", turning towards the rising sun like a sunflower (344) – the very movement of the CN Tower, « qui tient à ce que l'on reconnaisse son langage anti-Babel, sa *langue rocaille*, l'intimité du temporel dans l'immortel, l'Esprit-Orignal » (345; emphasis mine). While it is a return « au primordial... Tournés vers le Levant », it is not the romantic anti-technology pastoralism espoused by, for instance,

Norman Mailer. Rather, it would use technology to create and operate, not McLuhan's "global village", but the « "village-tour", pas la tour d'ivoire des intellectuels aigris qui ne font que macérer dans leur jargon abscons, mais le village qui offre à tous ses habitants des tours de travail, de loisir, de réflexion et d'action ... et entre toutes une tour culturelle pour délier la langue des précédentes » (345-46). Above all, there is language, and a natural language. Twylla stresses that « la nature, les animaux, les choses nous parlent mieux avec leur silence que les êtres qui vocifèrent leur savoir aux quatre coins de la planète... » (347). The word « silence » foreshadows the very end of the novel.

After this dialogue – no longer a *dialogue de sourds* – the Tower returns to frame the tale: « C'est un *scoop* pour moi, Tour CN, d'avoir capté et transcrit ce dialogue des profondeurs, le premier dans son genre. Les deux femmes ont parlé, ensemble, à cœur ouvert ... elle me comble de satisfaction parce qu'elle émerge de la pierre ! » (347). It is Twylla's love that enables the Tower to give birth to words: « J'ai accompli ce tour d'écorce verbale à la manière des bras de Twylla qui m'ont enlacée un jour. Non pas pour communiquer des informations sur ondes ou sur écrans, mais pour me transmettre son amour » (349).

The Immigrants: An "Anacharsis Klootz Deputation"

If it were not for these "privileged moments" of communion, Toronto, as well as the "global village",would remain an Eliot-esque "Waste Land", with the crowds emerging from the CN Tower and the Sky Dome resembling those crossing London Bridge, experiencing a death-in-life:

> Unreal City,
> Under the brown fog of a winter dawn,
> A crowd flowed over London Bridge, so many,
> I had not thought death had undone so many,
> Sighs, short and infrequent, were exhaled,
> And each man fixed his eyes before his feet. (I: 60-65)

Rocco: The Mediterranean

Of the three recent immigrants who stand out in the text, only one tries to embrace the capitalistic system, despite his own nature: Rocco Cacciapuoti, whose last name means "a seeker after power", and whose first name refers again to "rock" or stone. This "piccolo Napoleone" came to Canada seeking his own personal Eldorado, but adding to the mix his "Mediterranean blood giving zest to life" (104). The descendant of generations of masons, he becomes, ironically, an MP and Minister of Communications in a language he scarcely knows! Not to worry, he has succeeded a Ukrainian who, in turn, has succeeded a Pole. We are warned that he is tricky rather than genial, and he only "helps" Twylla in order to rid himself of her. His appointment results from a Liberal government's patronage, but he must move to the right if he has any hope of keeping his post: « *Mais le pouvoir me ligote et je ne peux rien décider par moi-même dans ce pays de liberté et de démocratie » (222).* An arriviste /opportunist, he does indeed lose his position in the Liberal caucus when he votes against the GST (231). He has already betrayed Pete by not pleading his cause, and compares himself to the traitor Count Ugolino della Gherardesa in Dante's *Inferno (*222).

The Tower comments that « Rocco n'a réussi dans le nouveau monde que parce qu'il porte en lui le monde ancien » (219). He constantly compares the Toronto cityscape to his native Italy: « Rien de la sorte autour de moi » (219). As the Tower remarks, the whole world swims in a sea of illusion, and the greatest illusion is that of Uniqueness (220). But at least Rocco assists the Tower to keep her illusions by sending Twylla to Malaysia. However, he doesn't even read her report, as he fails to intervene on Symphorien's behalf. The Tower privileges us to overhear a long soliloquy/monologue from Rocco, as from many of the other characters. He is at home in ambiguity, and only intervenes for others when there is something in it for himself. As an outsider, he recognizes that he will never be inside (« de souche »): « ... *vous n'êtes plus Italien et vous ne serez jamais Canadien* » in this "paradise"of « *souches élues* », the elect (226). He hears the majority culture telling him, « ... *nous sommes contre vous et nous n'aurons jamais confiance en vous* » (227). If he has cultivated the English language, it is because « *La première langue officielle ... est un peu moins chauvine que la deuxième* » (226). He licks his wounds like the she-wolf that nourished Romulus and Remus – another mother-image.

Rocco sees all his countrymen as « des Canadiens errants ». He uses the metaphor of writing, on a blank page, to suggest the country's racism: « *La page blanche doit "parler blanc", mais on n'a jamais su que le blanc a plusieurs teintes ! Qui sait que le blanc pur n'est qu'hérésie ? »* (226). In fact white, as Herman Melville points out in "The Whiteness of the Whale" in *Moby Dick (1851)*, has all the colors of the rainbow, and can be terrifying: it is "the colorless all-color of atheism". Rocco's status gives him a certain lucidity and clairvoyance as to Marc Durocher and the dream of Québec separation. Of the slogan, « *Un Québec souverain n'abandonnera pas les minorités francophones au Canada* », Rocco can only comment wryly, "Who are they kidding?" (225).

The Tower comments on Rocco's soliloquy, « sa propre autobiographie », admitting that this is not a subgenre she admires. But at least she is democratic: "They can't say that I don't allow my characters to express themselves" (231). She describes each character as an individual tower: « Tous mes personnages sont donc des parties de moi-même. Mais comme ils ont du caractère, ils deviennent autonomes. Chacun est une *tour* à son image » (244). But once created, they take on a life of their own, cut the umbilical cord: "There's nothing I can do". She claims she invented nothing. The characters « existent bel et bien et travaillent dans mon sein. Je les vois entrer et sortir en moi » (243).

Souleyman and Symphorien: Wise Man and "Holy Fool"

Two more appealing recent immigrants, from the Tower's point of view, are Souleyman Mokoko, from Africa, and Symphorien Lebreton, from metropolitan France.

Souleyman Mokoko, whom we meet first, is a black immigrant who climbs and descends the Tower, like Pete the Mohawk, but from the inside. He becomes its elevator operator, even though, as an "Engineer of bridges and roads", he is vastly overqualified (28). This is his first encounter with the subtle forms of Canadian racism – so subtle that Canadians themselves are often unaware of it: « ... il s'est trouvé monnaie non convertible dans ce pays d'accueil qui se targue d'être un des plus hospitaliers de l'Occident » (28). As a political refugee, he is ready, unlike Rocco Cacciapuoti, to embrace Canada wholeheartedly, and has no wish to return to the mother country. Souleyman and Pete, both colonized, but in different ways, become fast friends.

As his first name indicates, Souleyman has the wisdom of Solomon. Is he also the Nietzschean Superman, *sur-homme*, evoked, very differently, by Toni Morrison in her *Song of Solomon* (1977)? It also ties him to the unwise Pete, who nonetheless plays both Nietzschean and comic strip Superman in his leap from the Tower.

Souleyman speaks better French than Marcel-Marie Duboucher, who "butchers" the language (« bouche » also signifies "mouth"). The Tower thinks amusedly, comparing Souleyman to Marcel-Marie, French colonization succeeded better in Africa than in Canada. When the gay Marcel-Marie tries to seduce a Toronto French School student, the student and his teacher, to our great amusement, are more offended by the poor quality of his French than by his indecent approaches (53). Souleyman, on the other hand, is not only fluent in French, but « parfaitement bilingue » (54). This gift does not help him to secure steady employment in Canada; both he and Pete have no recourse but CUPE, a labor union determined mainly to protect the rules of seniority (54-55).

Like many immigrants of his race, whatever their nationality, he is relegated to the Jane-Finch corridor of North York (118). He loses his job, menial as it is, through no fault of his own. Leaving Jane-Finch for work, he loses control of his car on a sheet of black ice, creating a typical Toronto five-vehicle chain collision, which Bouraoui describes humorously in sexual terms: « Accident où la ferraille prend sa revanche dans une entre-pénétration jouissive » (181). Typically, too, Souleyman is blamed because of a series of stereotypes: « les Africains ne possèdent aucune notion du temps... Ils fabriquent des enfants qu'ils confient à la rue pour les élever... » (184). A Dr. Ronchon is quoted authoritatively: « *le cyperdépendant* – et tous ces Africains sont des cyperdépendants ! – *doit être traité comme l'alcoolique ou le toxicomane* » (184). Ironically, after his auto accident, Souleyman's next job is as a taxi driver, ferrying passengers to the CN Tower. The Tower's love of her characters is clear with Souleyman: « C'est vrai Souleyman ne me laisse pas indifférente » (183).

Souleyman's last name, Mokoko, sounds suspiciously like "Moki", Pete's and Twylla's son. In fact, Moki, from the north woods, teaches this man of the Sudan how to survive in Canada, snow-covered the better part of the year: « C'est le fils de Twylla, Moki, qui viendra le secourir et lui apprendre à vivre dans cet Igloo » (184).

If mothers and sons play significant roles in the narrative, so do at least one father and daughter (apart from Kelly and her father). Souleyman has a fifteen-year-old daughter, Amanicha, who, in fact, raises the questions of African and Egyptian history. The Egyptian references occur as early as Tour 3 when the Tower says, « ... toutes les collectivités se ressemblent depuis les Pharaons jusqu'à l'univers éclaté de cette fin de siècle » (36). Amanicha asks her father « pourquoi cette pyramide se termine-t-elle par une tête d'aiguille qui porte un turban ? » (185) – thus evoking the Egyptian pyramids of *La Pharaone.* If *La Pharaone* refers to Queen Hatchepsut,

Souleyman has had the idea of naming his daughter Amanicha for « la Reine Amanichakhéto » in their ancestral rich, powerful Kingdom of Koush (the Biblical Cush), which also expressed its worship in the mystic form of pyramids. Indeed, Souleyman admits that « ... la Tour est une pyramide en aiguille ... l'Aiguille rocheuse servait de symbole religieux pour les Pharaons » (186). The reference is to Cleopatra's Needle, also appropriated by Napoleon's armies. The Needle reminded Egyptians of both the eternal and the temporal, of immortality and mortality, of belief in God as well as temporality. It indicated origins, was fixed and immutable, while the CN Tower is a site of passage. But the Tower will establish her own claim to immortality: the "needle" is also the Tower's stem, or « tige », which she puns on, referring to her « vertige » and « prestige »: « Mon pouvoir donne le *vertige* et parfois le *prestige* » (119; emphasis mine). Thus, Pyramid and Tower seem both to become Jungian archetypes, part of some collective unconscious. Souleyman reminds his daughter that the CN Tower « n'est pas la même pyramide que celle dont je t'ai parlé. Et ce n'est pas un turban, c'est un cycle parfait » – like the Indian circle of life (185). Nonetheless, the Tower remains a kind of Rorschach test for the viewer, who sees it through the prism of his own culture. And the Tower herself is longing for some transcendent meaning, spirituality, « anti-Babel ».

Souleyman is not only a wise man, but a talespinner to his daughter, who asks him to tell her about their ancestral pyramids. What he recounts is the circularity of races and cultures, like those of individual men and women. The ancient Kingdom of Koush (Nubia, roughly corresponding to the modern Sudan), conquered Egypt: « Ses dynasties de Pharaons noirs venaient du Sud » (186). Now the former colonizer has become the colonized: « Nous avons été des conquérants et, à notre tour, nous avons été conquis » (186). Souleyman thus retraces and re-vises history, reminding his daughter of the former glories of black African civilization: from Djebel Barkal, "the Sacred Mountain", still today flanked by a rocky needle resembling this Tower, the Nubian princes of his people left to conquer Egypt. Souleyman's ancestors came from the Kingdom, now known as the Sudan, spread over the confluence of the White Nile, the Blue Nile and the Atbara. Dynasties of black Pharaohs came from the South. In the beginning (about 2500 B.C.), it was the independent kingdom Kerma – perhaps the most ancient in Africa (186). Moreover, according to one theory, the ancient Egyptians themselves may have been black. It is Souleyman, as well, who has a vision of a "Tour Multi-Cult" (247).

The CN Tower is flattered by all this attention. As Twylla imparts love and the Esprit-Orignal to her, Souleyman gives her history and another ancient mysticism: « ... il me plaît en effet de me voir, parmi les pyramides, une très haute pyramide » (189). Mystics have long believed in the magical powers of the pyramidal shape. And she values the fact that our Canadian "huddled masses" come to her to confide, as American immigrants, and their children, turn to the Statue of Liberty: « Il n'aurait jamais pu ouvrir son cœur de la sorte à un Canadien pelure de laine ou pureté de chevreau ! » (188). She is delighted to be compared to « l'aiguille rocheuse » or the « ventre de la pierre » Souleyman describes: « Du coup, je me suis vue installée dans une tradition millénaire. Grâce à cet étranger, devenu Canadien, qui ne trahit pas sa mémoire ! » (188).

Souleyman, now the proverbial Ph.D. driving a cab, holds no grudge against the Tower; to the contrary: « La Tour ne me trahit pas, mais ses *managers*. Eux ne l'emporteront pas au paradis ! » (188). Rather, he blames "the system": Kelly herself is but a cog in the wheel: « On ne peut rien y changer, même pas la graisse qui lubrifie *la machine infernale* » (190; emphasis mine), the last reference a nice bit of intertextuality, demonstrating Souleyman's familiarity with Jean Cocteau. If he no longer ascends and descends the Tower, Souleyman now constantly deposits visitors at her feet. And he wants to protect her: « ... j'ai créé une amulette *Tour-aiguille-Ventre-pierre* pour éloigner le mauvais œil de ma Tour CN » (191). The khamsa of *Bangkok Blues* serves the same purpose. Souleyman refers to his « tigritude rythmale », as to « Négritude », but also « tige » and, of course, « tigre ». He wants, above all, to give the Tower "a soul" (191). Some see him as an African magician or sorceror, and Bouraoui has him comment self-reflexively (on Bouraoui's own text, *La Rose des sables*): « Car dans le désert qui ne rejette personne, fleurissent et survivent, pour toujours, les plus belles roses de sable » (191).

Souleyman quotes Mohammed: « *Une pierre est descendue du ciel plus blanche que le lait, mais les péchés des hommes l'ont noircie* », a parable Souleyman applies to the CN Tower (191; emphasis mine). The Tower in turn recognizes that he had used his *black* hands in the elevator, to protect the Tower with *white* magic, a Melvillean play on our preconceptions of black and white, and their supposed associations with evil and good. Souleyman also notes the irony of scheduling the Black Festival, Kuumba, in February, the coldest, nastiest month of the year (190). Despite the view of Toronto as a whited sepulchre, for the most part the Tower recognizes her city as the most dynamic and cosmopolitan in the world., changed from 1950 (three-quarters of British origin) to today (three-quarters multicultural).

If Souleyman is the wise man, Symphorien Lebreton is the "wise fool" or "holy fool", speaking truth in nonsense. His first name suggests a symphony which is worth nothing, or comes to nothing – « Sympho-rien » – and his last name suggests his origins, a Breton from Brittany, the only native-born Frenchman in the narrative. Given his talents, there is also probably an echo of the surrealist André Breton. He is a half-crazed would-be poet, through whom Bouraoui manages to poke some good-natured fun at poets in general, with some self-reflexive irony directed at himself,[12] and at stereotypical audience responses, ranging from total indifference to suspicion to fear and loathing – fear, specifically, that he may be a terrorist who will blow up the Tower, and half of Toronto with it! Is Bouraoui thinking of the Breton movement for independence, and their fight to maintain their own (Celtic) language within France? Or of their historic link to Celtic Britain and Cornwall, bagpipes and all, associating them with both of the Founding Nations of Canada?

The Tower sees herself as Symphorien's mother, opening her arms in an embrace – no wonder, when we meet his formidable biological parent, Madame Lebreton, with her aggresstive epistolary style! And Symphorien reciprocates that love: « *Je t'aime Tour comme l'amour qui tourne au vinaigre. Pas comme cet Africain débarqué de la lune* » (199). But he also sees her in sexual terms: « *Dans tes entrailles, je me masturbe avec les mots... J'éjacule en toi mes paroles de pierre pour t'ensemencer de nouvelles lois d'hospitalité* » (200).

Symphorien appears relatively late in the narrative; he is named only on page 112, shortly following the Tower's perception, at the beginning of Tour 9, of an unknown « Intrus » (109). He is likened to Ralph Ellison's *Invisible Man*, also nameless at the start, who hides in a basement from the racist world of 1940s New York City, and cultivates Emersonian self-reliance to the point of plugging into the Monopolated Power and Light Company (Con Ed?). Trying to be invisible, however, Symphorien "sticks out like a sore thumb" (112). He is a black squirrel hiding his peanut, not in a tree trunk, but in the Tower's stairwell. His "peanuts" are *billets-doux*, the equivalent of Melville's Bartleby the Scrivener's "dead letters" (1856),

---

[12] Bouraoui has admitted in an interview that there may be an echo of himself, « mais peu importe ! »

or, more conspicuously, of Dr. Reefy's "paper pills", words of insight scribbled and crumpled in his pockets, in Sherwood Anderson's short story of the same name in *Winesburg, Ohio* (1919). The Tower is somewhat ambivalent about him. Sometimes he alarms her, but for the most part she realizes he has no bad intentions: « Il croit nourrir ainsi ma base, me gaver de ses mots-talismans, de ses bulles cérébrales... Mouvements intuitifs sans parole, sans musique, sans lumière » (112). He dreams of his words being carried throughout the world « dans les musées de l'imaginaire »[13]. The Tower (Bouraoui) then self-reflexively, and very humorously, notes, « Dès lors, il sera le lauréat du Prix Trillium » (112)[14]. We are reminded of Kateb, in *Retour à Thyna*, who hangs *his* "paper pills", in the form of poems, on the ficus trees along the boulevard.

The Tower and Symphorien are "in synch": « ... je me demande si mes vibrations n'ont pas déclenché son séisme ? » They play a cat-and-mouse game, and for the time being the Tower thinks that « Symphorien tient à démanteler le système que j'ai mis en place » (113). As the Tower says, however, "Nobody can fight City Hall" (113). She then humorously lists all the eccentrics who have tried to master her:

> *Il est vrai que je suis un aimant puissant qui attire les excentriques de tout poil. Des gens streaked down les 2570 marches de mes escaliers. Nus comme des vers luisants, dégringolant sexes à l'endroit et à l'envers. Certains se sont délibérément foulé la cheville ou cassé le pied pour des retours d'assurances assurés. Certains ont escaladé les marches en motos, avec des pogo sticks, charriant des pianos, des réfrigérateurs ou démontant une Jeep Suzuki. Tant d'autres exemples que je ne saurais mentionner. Par prudence et par objectivité. Notons, cependant, que Brendan Keenoy accomplit la montée la plus rapide – un record – en sept minutes cinquante-deux secondes, en 1989. On s'est jeté du Skypod avec ou sans câble. Remonté en araignée sur les fenêtres en verre à l'extérieur. Tout cela pour dire que chaque fois qu'il existe un record à établir, l'on va se précipiter pour l'annuler et prendre la place du premier.* (114)

Symphorien makes the Tower his nest, or home, made completely of paper: « Au milieu de ses meubles en papier, ses bibelots en papier, ses coussins en

---

[13] The « imaginaire » is Gilbert Durand's term for an interdisciplinary criticism examining the creative process.

[14] Pierre Léon's article, entitled « Avec un finaliste du prix Trillium, la Tour CN perd la tête », noting that this novel was indeed a Trillium Award finalist, concludes, « Un beau texte sur un pays en devenir. À lire en attendant...le Prix ? » (8).

papier, jusqu'à ses serviettes de toilettes et ses mouchoirs de papier ... il a l'air d'être lui-même une armature où la graphie justifie son existence, donne corps à ce décor fait maison » (117). His words are those of a man flayed alive, of an omniscient author addressing only himself. He utters equally words of hate and love, but there is no internal coherence: « On peut suivre les méandres de son écriture de chat cauteleux sans trouver leur cohérence, même s'ils biberonnent un chaos de sens capable de démanteler ma propre silhouette » (117).

Nonetheless, in the final analysis, the Tower appreciates Symphorien's contributions to her narrative: « ... je sens son désir ouater les traces de ma voix dans ce récit... » (117). She wonders still if he is planning to blow her up, « tirer sur la gâchette afin de bloquer le flux de mes images et me réduire au désespoir, au silence infini... » (118), an echo of Pascal's « Le silence infini de ces espaces éternels m'effraie ». Instead of "Thus Spoke Zarathustra", the Tower might be "speaking" Pascal.

She comes to realize, however, that Symphorien « m'est fidèle jusqu'à la nuque » (200). He seems a symphony conductor, or a musician, ranging from Pavarotti to Duke Ellington to the Platters: "Only you can make me believe..." (202-03). He even evokes Tchaikovsky's 1812 Overture: « Puis les deux mains de Symphorien marquent le silence, et dans un déchirement soudain qui fait secouer mes parois en verre, explose la colère des batteries, la violence éjaculatoire des cymbales. La foudre tombe du ciel » (201). At times he howls like a Northern wolf (203); at others he is Romeo, Mac the Knife, and Torero (204). Symphorien embodies some contradictions of the Canadian immigrant: « Volcan aux rares éruptions, Symphorien est un chaos de glace et de feu dont l'unique dessin est un « *dur* désir de *durer* » (202; emphasis mine). By now the Tower is shielding and protecting him. She recognizes that he is nothing like the "nut" who attacked tourists in the Empire State Building (204). But the Empire State Building couldn't tape what happened; the CN Tower is capable of registering everything: « ... mon antenne, à moi, est plus vigilante, probablement parce que je suis de nature plus réceptive » (205). She knows, however, that Symphorien is « bénin à la racine », and is only suffering from solitude – the Third Solitude of the recent immigrant. At the very end, she admits, « Je reviens à Symphorien parce que j'éprouve une certaine sympathie pour ce Français perdu. Je le dis sans ambage » (313).

The Francophones « de Souche »

Despite his recurrent obsessions which land him in mental institutions, and his *idée fixe* to carve out the owner's heart and brains (her machinery and stairwell), and create an Eiffel Tower in her place – as his mother lectures the Tower on classical French grammar – it isn't his Cartesianism that succeeds in planting a bomb. Rather, an explosion is caused by the two idiots *de souche*, Marc Durocher and Marcel-Marie Duboucher, whom it is difficult to tell apart (like any two of the Three Stooges), and who seem to disappear from the latter part of the text until their attempted coup. At the end Symphorien is merely facing east – the Eiffel Tower – in a position of worship (249). As Bouraoui notes, Madame Lebreton says, « Il ne faut pas malmener ma langue », which is ironic since the Tower is capable of assimilating and disseminating *all* languages, because love masters all languages. Thus, the Tower has sympathy for the alienation of the Lebretons, but she transcends their French chauvinism.

The Tower: A Female Quest

Marc and Marcel-Marie, on the other hand, as alike as two peas in a pod, do not particularly interest Bouraoui – or the Tower – probably because they are too local, particularized. At the very end the Tower summarizes the various quests of the different characters:

> Je vois Rocco repartir en quête de son particularisme méditerranéen, Kelly de son lesbianisme souterrain et de son anglomanie englobante, Marc de son séparatisme décadent, Marcel-Marie de sa souchitude rampante, Souleyman de sa tigritude reconciliante et Symphorien de sa scribouillerie qui se love à l'intérieur. (329)

But the Tower herself has been on a quest. This notion may seem a contradiction in terms, since she is rooted in concrete and cannot move in a linear direction. But her quest is circular, turning a full 360 degrees in an hour, and is parallel to the circular quest of the Amerindian Twylla, and the Malaysian Zinal (or the quest of Mansour and Zitouna through octopus-shaped Thyna). Perhaps the quest needs to be redefined in non-Occidental terms. It is an Amerindian-Oriental-female quest. Indeed, the Tower fulfills a spiritual quest through Twylla and the Esprit-Orignal, Zinal and the Menara Tower, Souleyman and the pyramids.

Thus the novel goes well beyond Margaret Atwood's survival motif – « car survivre est la quête canadienne par excellence » – to a Faulknerian certainty that "man [woman] will not only endure; [s]he will prevail". [15]

The Tower takes us into her confidence as narrator: « ... je me demande comment je vais terminer mon histoire ? » (329), which she qualifies as a « récit-roman-journal-prosème » (348). She reminds us that « Des mains autochtones et des mains venues du monde entier m'ont érigée » (314). Her greatest sympathies are clearly for *« nous, Africains, Afro-Américains, Antillais, Autochtones ... et autres premières lettres de l'Alphabet »* (328). For the most part her characters speak in monologues because solitude is universal: « Les gens sont cloîtrés dans une tragique solitude » (347), and this is a state she wants to transcend by creating a « littérature d'orignalitude ». She becomes a great mother figure, an umbilical cord for her characters. Now she is going to free them to find their own way: « ... je vais couper le cordon, me fracturer en mots-rocailles... » (349).

Beginning the new millennium, the Tower affirms the connection between herself and speech: « Pierre de souche, Tour de touche, je suis la carte d'identité de la Ville-Reine ». Now twenty-five ears old,[16] « Morte pour l'un, je ressusciterai pour le suivant... Mais existerai-je si mon histoire n'est pas maintenant racontée ? Au fond, qu'est-ce qu'une tour qui n'inspire ni légende ni conte, ni même le courroux des mauvaises langues ? » (291). Zarathustra, too, uttered wisdom from his tremulous stone lips, but, as Bouraoui notes, he "spoke" in the past tense, while the Tower speaks in the present, and looks to the future.

The Tower has found its legend, embodied in this lyric novel which offers a vision of liberty and tolerance, a dream for all people who shelter in this Canada, from the original inhabitants, the Amerindians

---

[15] In fact, Bouraoui doesn't hesitate to critique the *Survival* thesis humorously: « ... *Survival*, sur laquelle l'écrivaine Margaret Atwood a mis le doigt pour délier tant de bourses... *Souchique* en son âme et conscience, sa parole devient l'essence de notre sagesse et de notre identité » (156-57).

[16] Bouraoui has mentioned that the Tower's existence in Canada is just a little shorter than his own.

and Inuit, to the founding nations, French and British, to the recent immigrants[17]. All these are embraced by the spirit of « Orignalitude », « une source d'inspiration, un souffle constant de tolérance, une manière d'être laïque et républicaine » (292). After all the verbal fireworks, power, lyricism, studied multilingualism, when and if the vision is fulfilled, the rest is « silence », the last word of the novel ... or the Word Made Stone![18]

---

[17] The Tower stresses all along the differences between the Canadian treatment of immigrants, the cultural mosaic, and the American, the melting pot: « ... nous n'avons fait bouillir les immigrés dans le *Melting pot* américain pour les niveler au ras des pâquerettes, *the American way of life*" (39). [A first-year Humanities student actually used this phrase to define "melting pot": "When the immigrants come to America they put them in this big pot and boil them"]. She sees this Canadian policy as a « Ruée vers *l'or du temps* », incidentally a reference to the name of Bouraoui's Tunisian publisher (39; emphasis mine).

[18] Unfortunately, the Canadian editor omitted the last turn of the Tower, Tour 24, signifying twenty-four hours of turning per diem. It consisted of a blank page, à la Laurence Sterne's *Tristram Shandy*, indicating the Tower's silence, but inviting the reader to complete the work. The twenty-four Tours are designed to correspond to twenty-four hours in the life of Toronto, analogous to Joyce's *Ulysses*, spanning twenty-four hours in the life of Dublin. Except for that last missing Tour, I can see only one other number that is significant, Tour 13, a mystic number, in which Twylla goes into a trance and has her vision. The Tunisian editor, incidentally, did include the last Tour, but headed it Tour 00 for the year 2000, also missing the point of the blank page and the significance of 24.

roman

Hédi Bouraoui

La composée

V

La Composée :

Or, The Muse Strikes Back

In *La Composée* (2001), we move from a talking Tower to a heroine of flesh and blood who is, nonetheless, like the CN Tower, on a quest for identity. There is no double heroine this time, but a singular being viewed from the outside (until the end) and interpreted by a series of males. Though the novel begins in Paris, « La Ville-Lumière », her identity quest focuses on a city by the sea, Marseille. But the mystery deepens, and is finally resolved, on a historic Tunisian island. As in the previous novels, space and time are closely linked, for on this island steeped in the past, she finds her own roots.

At the beginning, one expects *La Composée* to be another romantic novel focusing on male perspectives on an enigmatic Muse. Even the cover illustration suggests a jigsaw puzzle to be pieced together by the male gaze. She wears a Mona Lisa smile, or perhaps the archaic smile of ancient Greek and Etruscan statues. The smile, however, hints at hidden knowledge which the supposed "Muse" possesses, mocking the obtuseness of her male admirers.

By the end, the "Muse" turns the tables, and proves to be herself the authentic artist. Taking pen in hand, she tells her own story, demolishing the other hypothetical versions of "truth" the male point of view characters present. It is interesting too that she moves back to the epistolary form, typical of the eighteenth century and the beginnings of the novel, a new form in which women began to gain the confidence to move from private sphere (journals and letters) to publication (the novel)[1]. She is thus in many ways the culmination of Bouraoui's previous female protagonists. If Koï represents the gaps, the silences in which the male artist finds his voice, Zitouna adopts the male role of talespinner. Hatchepsut composes her fourteen tablets without publicly acknowledging her authorship, and Francine pieces together the fragments of Barka Bousiris's writings, probably adding her own creative vision, but giving all the credit to him. Twylla Blue expresses herself mystically and through soapstone sculptures, while the CN Tower, in adopting a female voice, becomes « Anti-Babel » and tries to set in order the postmodern chaos of telecommunications. Héloïse, « la Composée », subverts male observers/narrators, and becomes herself the narrator of her life.

This tight, compressed little novel is a real tour de force with surprises around every corner. In the final analysis, the composition becomes herself the composer, multicultural, of unknown parentage on the father's side, embodying three major religions, and who effects a personal quest for her cultural, national, religious roots.

The structure is triadic, focusing on three principal characters: Samir Arhab, the young Tunisian restaurateur with literary pretensions; Jean-Marc Léger, the aged Don Juan/poet; and Héloïse Orsini-Uzan, the object of both their male gazes, who has more than a few ideas of her own. There is also Ali Ben Mokhtar, another aged writer, but Arabo-musulman, on the island of Djerba. He seems to function as another version of Jean-Marc, from another culture and religion. The inscrutable Héloïse doesn't make her dramatic entrance until page 55, chapter 5, more than midway through the text, but she is present by her absence throughout the earlier portion when she is the object of speculation (and composition) on the part of Jean-Marc and Samir.

Jean-Marc Léger: The Sly Old Fox

To begin at the beginning, Héloïse is first presented from the point of view of Jean-Marc Léger. He is the narrator, Samir Arhab the *narrataire*, or

---

[1] See Virginia Woolf, *A Room of One's Own* (1929). As the philosopher Alain Touraine has also remarked, the history of the novel corresponds to the history of women.

listener. Samir falls in love (or so he thinks) with the fantasy figure of Héloïse as constructed by Jean-Marc, who at least knows her. This figure is deconstructed by Samir who doubts the older man's veracity, and then reconstructed by Samir to fit his own fantasies.

Jean-Marc Léger is an aged poet of considerable charm but less talent, as his last name, "lightweight", suggests. He takes pride in « son moi charmeur et donjuanesque » (9), and he courts women, including, supposedly, Héloïse, with his poems, conveyed effectively by « le timbre sensuel de sa voix » (40). Héloïse is « la nouvelle Nouvelle Héloïse », a postmodernist version of Rousseau's eighteenth-century heroine Julie, the quintessential Romantic heroine, virtuous but sensual; however, she is also the archetypal medieval Héloïse. Jean-Marc sees himself as her « Abélard des temps nouveaux » (11). Samir thinks to himself, who's he kidding? an old man, probably impotent, putting himself in the position of the medieval Héloïse's learned mentor and lover. Héloïse does, in fact, resemble more the medieval prototype than Rousseau's Julie in that she rejects dependency on a man and carves her own niche, as the medieval Héloïse became an abbess, a scholar, and an early feminist heroine.

Samir sees that Jean-Marc has built castles in Spain. Together they are a kind of Bouvard and Pécuchet à la Flaubert, representing young and old (15). Jean-Marc, the first narrator of the text, introduces the theme of Héloïse's love for the *mère-patrie*, Tunisia, and the island of Djerba in particular. He sees that she has cut the umbilical cord tying her to her mother, the Corsican Marie Orsini, but not the link to her native land. Jean-Marc compares her suggestively to Samir, who is also tied to his mother, whom, nevertheless, he hasn't seen in ten years, and the motherland which, however, he visits only rarely and reluctantly. For Héloïse's parents, a Corsican and a Tunisian Jew, « ce pays ... n'était pas le leur, mais ... les a marqués jusqu'à la moëlle épinière » (14).

Jean-Marc's balcony, which overlooks Paris and « les splendeurs de la Ville Lumière » (19), prefigures the balcony of Room 305 at the hotel "Elmansiya" at Taguermess on the isle of Djerba which Héloïse visits again and again in quest of her origins, and which overlooks the blue Mediterranean.

In effect, by chapter 2 Héloïse has "dumped" Jean-Marc, whatever their real relationship is, because he becomes possessive: « Elle dit que je suis exigeant » (20). We learn her side to this story only later in the tale. Jean-Marc falls into a decline or depression, no longer reads poems, and says, « je n'ai plus rien à dire » (25). Three days later – again the mystic number – he falls victim to gastroenteritis, and three days after that he is dead, shuffled quickly off this mortal coil by the author. He is buried in Père Lachaise Cemetery, and Samir begins to wonder if Héloïse has killed him (31). He also begins to wonder, did Jean-Marc fabricate « son dernier amour en bordure de mort » (31)?, and refers to it as « l'amour crépusculaire » (32).

Samir Arhab: Prince Charming and the Sleeping Beauty

Samir Arhab's last name creates all sorts of problems for him in his adopted country, France, but in Arabic it means not "Arab", but « Bienvenue », "Welcome". His "welcome" in France, however, is problematical. The French Jean-Marc translates Samir's first name into Sam, which would be Samuel, and therefore Jewish, symbolically suggesting the wedding of cultures at the heart of this text.

Samir's fantasy seems drawn from the world of fairy tales (Occidental), or the Thousand and One Nights (Oriental). The Western fairy tale frame, à la Charles Perrault, however, prevails, as he values France over Tunisia. He sees himself as Prince Charming waiting in the wings to awaken with a kiss Sleeping Beauty, the Belle of the Woods.

Samir is very skeptical about the tale of the Belle as filtered through his aging friend. He thinks unflatteringly, « Arrête tes effusions lyriques » (12), and doubts this exaggerated story. He helps the old man make dinner, preparing the tomato salad to give a little respite to Jean-Marc's prolix discourse. He suspects that Héloïse could only be Jean-Marc's mistress out of self-interest (15). Above all, he wants direct access to the Belle's own discourse. As the old saying goes, beware lest you get what you wish for. He finally accesses her language with a vengeance! Her direct discourse comes in the form of a long letter in which she rejects him, just as she has rejected Jean-Marc.

He identifies with her in part because they were both born on the island of Djerba, *l'Île des lotophages* in Homer's Odyssey, or the Island of Forgetfulness where Ulysses nearly forgets his mission, is deflected from it. The hotel Elmansiya means literally « L'Oubliée », and Samir's project becomes a reconstitution of Héloïse's past, thereby leading to a measure of control over her and over himself: « En réalité, ne sommes-nous pas tous en train de vivre dans l'illusion suprême de contrôler plus ou moins notre sort ? » (32).

Samir thinks of himself accordingly as a self-made man, « Créé de toutes pièces ! » But in effect we are all the products of our history, even when we least suspect it. A would-be poet himself, he has earned by hard work a Bac de Lettres Modernes in Tunis. But he becomes an entrepreneur, moving from tour guide to restaurant dishwasher, to cook, to waiter, to co-owner. He perfects his knowledge of the language of Molière and Racine while neglecting his own. If he tries to forget his culture, Héloïse tries to remember hers. He thinks he has "composed" himself, whereas he has allowed himself to be shaped by the Occident, while repudiating his own culture. He writes a « poésie de mauvais aloi », even dedicating a long poem to Paris, ironically praising her welcoming qualities and her cultural riches (33).

He completes his cultural assimilation by forming a liaison with a Frenchwoman, Véronique Fournier from Normandy, « Française de France » (evoking Françoise and Francine, but we never get to know her). After living together for five years more or less amicably, they finally marry, but her parents insist she keep her maiden name because to call herself Madame Arhab would be to « s'attirer tous les ennuis du monde » (33). Living together was fine, but the marriage lasts only two years: « les deux années de vie conjugale furent un enfer de querelles et de contestations » (34). The trade-off is that he helps her buy a partnership in a law firm, while she helps him obtain French citizenship. She takes another lover, « un Juif électricien au chômage, tout en se jurant de ne plus commettre l'erreur fatale du mariage ».

Samir is torn between two cultures. On the one hand, he thinks that in his adoptive country, he was swimming better than a fish in water. On the other hand, his immersion is compared to a bath « dans son huile d'olive importée de Tunisie sous un prestigieux label italien... » (34). He refuses to change his name to Jean-Marie Dupont (pont = bridge), because he was proud of « ses origines africaine, maghrébine, tunisienne... » (35). He recalls the anecdote of little Mohamed whose teacher advises him to change his name to Lucien, at which point his Maghrebian parents hit the roof – and him. His explanation to his teacher shows an extreme dissociation from his own roots: « ... j'ai été agressé par deux Arabes ! » (36). Samir accepts at the most the abridgment of his first name to "Sam" « pour l'alléger de son ire ! » (37).

His ties to his mother – and *mère-patrie* – are equally ambivalent. He spoils his father until his death, loves his mother, but doesn't see her for ten years. He sends her money and phones her twice a month, when she always repeats the same litany – return home and marry a Tunisian woman: « Ma mère est une véritable poétesse sans le savoir... Le soleil, le ciel et la mer éparpillent ses vers au gré des vents de la prière ! » (37). She tries to matchmake and he bends the truth slightly by telling her he is already interested in « une femme née dans notre pays », without mentioning her mixed ethnic background (38). At times, when he thinks of the supposedly bizarre couple of Jean-Marc and Héloïse, he senses his imbalance, « un déséquilibre existentiel pareil à celui de ce couple étrange » (29). Why "existential"? Perhaps in the sense of his precarious self-determination, self-composition.

Samir consciously rejects his native land: « ... il cultive un détachement forcené pour ne pas succomber à l'amertume et aux récriminations ». He claims that he will never return after his mother dies: « Je n'y ai plus rien à branler ... ni soleil, ni mer, ni ciel bleu, ni jasmin, ni thé à la menthe ! » His reductive mockery of Maghrebian life is contrasted sharply to his paradisiac vision of France, as fantastic as his dream vision of Héloïse: « ... vivre à l'étranger, c'est jouir d'un paradis terrestre de son vivant, sans attendre celui de l'au-delà » (33). Even his sister, in Tunisia, prefers French candy to the native delicacies! Samir – and Bouraoui – seem to think, however, things are changing.

But Samir does return to Tunisia, and Djerba, in search of the mysterious Héloïse. He returns in the off-season, the winter, to reconnoiter. Does he rediscover his own country through her? Even in his dreams, however, all scenarios « finissent toujours par les dérobades de la femme désirée » (39) – and the reader is left to wonder if he really wants consummation, since the real never corresponds to the ideal. On his return, he finds Djerba in a complete state of touristic expansion, with its Cafétéria Lotus, its Laboratory Control, and palatial Royal Beach Hotel. He is proud that the island « a quintuplé en expansion féroce » (42), but he is also relieved to see that the modest old hotel Elmansiya has retained its intimate air. He considers Djerba the most beautiful island in the world, and the sea is always present, « triomphante par son éternelle présence » (43). He imagines Héloïse as a mermaid, « une daurade-sirène », or as Botticelli's Venus rising from the waves on her shell. On the balcony of the very room 305 which she usually reserves, « ... il s'imagine en train de dialoguer avec celle qui a surgi toute ruisselante de la mer pour l'étreindre dans ses bras » (45). Like the most famous visitor to the island, Ulysses, he feels that he is on the road to discovery. His quest also evokes memories of the mother and the Turkish bath, the *hammam*, which became a kind of childhood initiation into sensuality. He admits that « Seules les femmes tunisiennes savent exhiber cette lascivité débridée » (39), and he wonders if a *hammam* was also responsible for Héloïse's supposed voluptuousness, a ritual « d'où Héloïse émergeait, peu à peu, chair irisée, née des effluves et de la rosée » (44).

Samir plays the role of detective at the hotel, questioning the proprietor, the maid, the housekeeper, the old writer, until his family comes to absorb him: « ... l'enquête l'attend ! » (45). He spends three days there, again the mystic number, but his detective work in search of « la princesse Héloïse » is somewhat haphazard, fatalistic: « ... il décide de laisser le hasard faire les choses, comme tout bon fataliste du coin » (45).

The proprietor, who is, typically, rarely on site, alleges confidentiality when questioned, and asks Samir who he is in any case. Samir replies philosophically, quoting Montaigne, as though there is unconscious truth in jest: « Qui suis-je ? Éternelle quesion dont personne ne peut faire le tour même jusqu'à la mort » (46). The proprietor accuses him of falling in love with a dream, a woman he doesn't know from Adam or Eve. He is more acute than he realizes, for Samir wants to see Héloïse as the princess, the « Belle au bois veillant » (48). But he denies to the proprietor that she is only a dream, for « ... Héloïse existe bel et bien. Elle a mon âge, s'occupe d'architecture, revient dans son pays natal » (47). The proprietor at this point slips up, falls into the trap, and admits that she is « engagée dans le projet du Musée des Arts et des Civilisations à Paris ».

From his various sources Samir "composes" a picture of Héloïse. He learns that her name in Tunisian is Khaoukha (a peach), and that her surname is Uzan. Her father was a Tunisian Jew, David Uzan, whose name in Tunisian translates as Ouazzane (peseur). « Peseur » is opposed to « Léger », the other father-figure, Jean-Marc. Her mother was a Corsican Catholic, Marie Orsini, and thus Héloïse was the product of two minority groups within a largely Islamic country. Her birthdate is not given, but Jean-Marc (who should know) says on the very first page of the novel that she is about forty at that time, but appears thirty. Twylla Blue becomes a mature woman in the course of the novel, but Héloïse is mature and self-aware from the start. Samir summarizes his findings on her identity: « La « Pêche qui pèse » lui va comme le gant: elle est assez belle, juteuse comme le fruit, ne prend les décisions qu'après avoir bien pesé le pour et contre. Son signe du zodiaque doit être Balance » (or Libra, the scales) (48).

The hotel staff all see in her a half-mystical devotion to her mother country (50). It seems to have become a kind of substitute religion in this woman, who is « *Djerbiya* de père en fille » (49): « ... la nostalgie... brûlait en elle comme un cierge dans une cathédrale bien fréquentée » (48-9). If the "cathedral" image evokes Christianity, however, we are reminded that Tunisia consists of « les diverses communautés religieuses, ethniques, culturelles [qui] ont vécu dans une harmonie et une tolérance exemplaires » (49)[2]. And Héloïse empathizes with all these communities. The aged writer who frequents the hotel and its surroundings, identified later as Ali Ben Mokhtar, the Arabo-musulman version of Jean-Marc Léger, hints that Héloïse may have « des liens cachés » with Djerba – and, as it turns out at the end, he should know.

An illiterate housekeeper provides Héloïse's business card which, of course, she cannot read:

Héloïse Orsini
Architecte-Peintre
12, Rue Louis Salvador
13006-Marseille. (51)

We learn only later why she seems to have taken her Corsican mother's name, Orsini, rejecting her father's Uzan or Ouazzane. "Mission accomplished", says Samir – but the hardest part of the mission, the encounter, is yet to come, and at Marseille.

Why has Héloïse chosen Marseille over Paris? Among many reasons, it is the port of entry for new immigrants to France from the South, particularly North Africa. It is situated on her beloved Mediterranean Sea, and celebrates twenty-six centuries of existence as « une métropole euroméditerranéenne ». Its vistas are virtually limitless, « cette cité tentaculaire [like Thyna/Sfax] à perte de vue. Seuls le port et la mer en marquent la limite ». The old port is the « cœur-joyau de la cité phocéenne où débute la fameuse Cannebière ». But Marseille is also the birthplace of the French Revolution, where Rouget de l'Isle composed « La Marseillaise » during the people's march on Paris.

Samir, in turn, hopes to accomplish his own « révolution tranquille » in Marseille, midway between the North (Paris) and the South (Tunisia). His choice of Marseille is thus in part geographical and political, and in part personal. He has two reasons to settle there: « ... y établir un commerce, et essayer de dénicher l'Héloïse de ses rêves » (53), thus combining love and

---

[2] Bouraoui has noted in a radio interview that Tunisia is « un carrefour de races et de religions », and that there were never any pogroms in Tunisia, nor violence stemming from religion.

economics (an unlikely marriage suggesting much of what is wrong with Samir's vision). He opens a restaurant called Le Caméléon in the quarter of Notre-Dame-du-Mont. Both names can be applied to Héloïse, a chameleon par excellence, who is also our lady on a pedestal for Samir.

He begins to put foot in mouth from the very beginning of his arranged first meeting with Héloïse in Marseille. Why, the reader wonders, does he need two other men (always a threesome) to meet her, instead of having the courage to make the overtures himself? It seems as if he needs a buffer zone, in the form of André, who scouted out a place for him in Marseille, and Mabrouk, his new associate, both of whom, we learn later, assume that she is an easy mark, and try to win her from their supposed "friend". Samir orders red wine with fish, and toasts « À nos amours et à notre amitié », ironic on both counts (59). We wonder, as well, whether she is more annoyed by his drinking wine in violation of his supposed religion, or by his poor taste in ordering the wrong wine!

Her letter setting forth all the obstacles to a relationship between them, her disappointment at his conduct and that of his friends, « *les deux mousquetaires* », traumatizes him – for all of three days (again!) which he spends in his room eating nothing but bread and oil and olives. He feels as if he were in a desert inundated by a sudden flood. The image conjured up is of the Biblical forty days' flood, and now he perceives « une Héloïse nouvelle sur les rivages » (76). After three sleepless nights, however, he says, « Demain, il fera jour ! » And we have the sense that Héloïse has taken the entire *malentendu* more seriously than he has.

On his return to Tunisia, Ali Ben Mokhtar (Mokhtar means "the chosen one") fills in more of the outlines of Héloïse's history. Known as « la conque de Djerba », he is a well of knowledge and anecdotes (76). He does not make a living from his writing, but from the courses he teaches. He writes everything down to settle every question, and clearly echoes Jean-Marc Léger, whom he nonetheless describes as « ce croulant ». Samir has to remind him, as he did Jean-Marc, « pas de poésie, s'il vous plaît ! » (80). Samir and Ali Ben Mokhtar discuss the French influence – « leur camembert culturel » (79), their « monologue à sens unique » (80). Ali Ben Mokhtar admits, however, that « le litige colon-colonisé [see Memmi, Fanon, *et al.*] est mort et enterré ! Il reste l'Histoire avec un grand H » (80).

Ali Ben Mokhtar claims that Héloïse's semitic roots, on the father's side if not the mother's, created a daughter who is « ultra-sensible, super-susceptible, d'humeur si changeante que le moindre mot peut l'expédier au septième ciel ou en enfer » (80). Her father could be Jewish or Arab, he says cryptically – later we guess the truth. If Héloïse began with « un attachement presque maladif au père », that father soon became a God of wrath, and she sided with the mother instead. David Uzan, though Tunisian, opposed independence from France, and fought the Arabs in Palestine. His motto was « L'année prochaine à Jérusalem », adapting the title of « L'Année dernière à Marienbad », a film based on illusion and interlocking narratives, like the dream of a singular Jerusalem. He fought in the Six Days War in 1967, but as a Sephardic Jew was given no respect or honors but military by Israel. In October 1973 he died fighting against the Arabs. Marie Orsini, on the other hand, though Corsican, sided with the Tunisians in their fight for independence[3]. Héloïse, like Marie and like Ali Ben Mokhtar, recognizes that truth is not the exclusive property of any individual, or any religion. Her mother believed in « la plénitude divine » (echo of Derrida?). Ali Ben Mokhtar admits, « Je connaissais bien Marie Orsini » (83), and we begin to wonder how well he knew her. Samir becomes jealous of Ali Ben Mokhtar, as he had been of Jean-Marc, and begins to suspect he could be Héloïse's real father (84).

The watercolor, a seascape, in the famous Room 305 suggests to Samir a projected exhibition of Héloïse's work at the hotel, which would reestablish contact with her. He looks towards « un nouvel art-poème », linking visual and verbal art. His mother, with her typical Tunisian *dictons*, warns him to open his ears to the *sea*, and to watch where he steps (87; emphasis mine).

There follow three years of complete silence on the part of Héloïse. He tries to trace her through the Rabbi of the synagogue where she painted a fresco. The rabbi not only denigrates her art, which is abstract (Arabic), but also sees her as a woman with problems who foments discord everywhere (90). He calls her the *Belle du Seigneur*, reinforcing Samir's own idea of her, but the Rabbi apparently means a kind of *Belle Dame sans Merci*. He quotes her disapprovingly, without understanding her thirst for lived experience: « Je ne mourrai pas de nostalgie pour quelque chose que je ne vivrai pas dans cette vie » (90). At Djerba « Toutes les portes demeurent closes », like the door of Jerusalem in her fresco. Thus on both the

---

[3] Bouraoui has remarked on the apparent timeliness of the novel, with its linkage of terrorism, war, and religion. But it was composed years before September 11, 2001, and the aftermath (radio interview).

personal and political levels – and the personal is the political – there is no outlet, or "no exit » in the Sartrean sense..

Samir memorizes the letter of rupture she has written to him after the frustrating meeting in Marseille: « Il ne la lit plus. Il la connaît par cœur » (90). He learns her marital history from her shoe salesman: she married a soldier when she was not yet twenty years old. He lived in a bunker designed to safeguard state secrets, and heads of state in the event of war. It is a banal story: he was unfaithful to her, and she attempted suicide (like Francine in the earlier novel), thus repeating her negative experience with the father (s).

Samir eventually receives a cryptic prose poem from Stavanger, Norway, presumably from Héloïse, giving the title of the novel in its masculine form, for it refers to Samir as « *le* Composé »: « Cherche, ô toi, le Composé de terre, d'huile et de bouchées d'oublis !/ ... /Ne se cristallise l'amour que sur le dos d'éclairs et de tonnerres » (92). Unable to decrypt it, he begins to forget her and to seek his sexual pleasures « auprès de conquêtes plus faciles », remembering that he has « un charme fou pour attirer à lui toutes les femmes qu'il désirait » (92). Thus, he sleeps around to forget his ideal love, and she is once again betrayed by a man. The novel ends with his mother's display of a picture, seemingly of a sunset, given to her by Samir's sister, and which she hangs despite the fact that the only other decorations she has are verses of the Koran. Samir discovers Héloïse's new signature on it, Héla Ben Mokhtar, identifying the true father (factual, spiritual, or both)? In the last line of the book, he says to himself, « Voici enfin ma Boîte noire », the record discovered after the crash of an airplane, as opposed to Virgulius's hopeful takeoff at the end of *Bangkok Blues*. If he has finally broken the code, metaphorically, it is only through his own self-destruction (or implosion). As Bouraoui puts it, "he crashes and burns ».

La Nouvelle Nouvelle Héloïse: The Female Quest

When we finally "meet" Héloïse in person, we are faced with a choice between the tragic medieval Héloïse and the romantic eighteenth-century Julie of Rousseau. Jean-Marc, who introduces her character, somewhat misses the point by evoking « tous les échos littéraires autour de l'héroïne de Rousseau » (11). His reading focuses on « la tendresse partagée », and certainly René Girard's concept of "triangular desire" comes into play in this text, as in most of Bouraoui's novels, with Jean-Marc, Samir, and Héloïse (as well as her mother's supposed love affairs). But "triangular desire" defines male desire in this novel, not the essence of Héloïse, who veritably has a program of her own.

Jean-Marc provides Samir with a bare outline of her life: born in Djerba, the only daughter of parents in business, she moved to Rouen at a young age. She lost her father in 1973, her mother in 1975. She was married once, at Saint-Mandé. We learn two unusual facts about her: she studied architecture, a profession and training notoriously exclusive of women, and she is on a quest, by way of the hotel Elmansiya at Taguermess, on the fertile plains of the island of Djerba. While Elmansiya means « L'Oubliée », the forgotten one, in Arabic, she is trying to remember: « ... c'est tout à fait logique de revenir sur les traces de sa naissance » (16). On Djerba, the Isle of the Lotus-eaters, Héloïse paradoxically cultivates her memory. Samir sees her, according to her representation by Jean-Marc, as a new Eve losing her innocence to a Maghrebian culture he considers alien to her: « ... la belle créature a de bons sentiments pour la culture étrangère infiltrée en elle comme le Serpent ravissant à Ève sa pudeur virginale » (17).[4]

Her father was Jewish, but « plus français que les Français »,while her mother, « catholique, soutenait les Arabes contre les colons » (20-1). Her family left Tunisia when she was ten, but no one forced them to leave. Her mother was one of those Mediterranean women who seem submissive, but are actually in control behind the scenes. She could say, « Je fais tourner mon *hommelette* autour de mon petit doigt » (22; emphasis mine). « *Hommelette* » is, of course, a pun on "little man", and « omelette ». In other words, she handles her man as deftly as she does her cooking. Jean-Marc reminds her of her father, and may in fact be her real father: « Elle ne pouvait que l'aimer et le haïr intensément » (22). In other words, her relations with the patriarchy are, at best, ambivalent.

Samir and Jean-Marc wonder exactly what she hopes to find on her balcony facing the sea in her hotel in Djerba, a site from which she has been absent since the age of ten. Is she « à la recherche du temps perdu »? Does she await « la bouteille jetée de l'autre côté de la Méditerranée »? (25).

---

[4] The philosopher Alain Touraine suggests an analogy between the struggle for cultural rights and the women's movement, an analogy which dominates Bouraoui's text.

Is she returning to the scene of the crime? If so, what crime? As Samir thinks, « Quelque chose de son pays natal doit la hanter » (25).

After Jean-Marc's death, she becomes mute for Samir, and thus even more enigmatic: « ... elle se mue en degré zéro de l'oralité [echo of Barthes], ne rapportant plus les faits et gestes d'une *charmante héroïne* de rêves » (31). *L'Inconnue/L'Oubliée* becomes a ghost for him: « Spectre récalcitrant à prendre forme. Se manifestera-t-elle en chair et en os en revenant à ce lieu dit *L'Oubliée* ? » (41). One can see Samir falling in love with a product of his own narcissism. He sees her as a new Penelope awaiting passionately the return of Ulysses (41). Elsewhere he calls her *la Fileuse*: « Tricote-t-elle dans le loisir des vacances, avec nonchalance, un destin qu'elle laisserait entrevoir à quelques privilégiés de son île natale ? » (41). Penelope, of course, was never on Djerba; it was Ulysses who was detained there, at risk of forgetting his quest, Penelope, and all else. Penelope was sitting at home awaiting his return, holding off suitors by successively knitting and unraveling her handiwork. In *La Composée*, it seem as if Héloïse is a female Ulysses on a female quest on *l'Île des lotophages*, but seeking remembrance instead of oblivion. It is revealing of his limitations that Samir's reference to Penelope reduces her to an image of passive submission and waiting.[5]

Finally Héloïse enters in person in Chapter 5, more than halfway through the book. She is described, but vaguely: mid-height, dressed in black, chestnut slacks, sunglasses. It is a cold winter day in Marseille: « Le mistral souffle un air glacial » (55). Samir, accompanied by his buffer of two friends, gets dizzy on meeting her: « Débordante affection qui l'étonne et le comble » (56). They cover each other with kisses in « la nudité d'un non-dit », while the two friends, amazed, are struck speechless. They think they are witnessing a « liaison dangereuse interrompue depuis quelque temps » (56). The *trois mousquetaires* echo the three principal characters. The passion of Samir and Héloïse is described as « écumes du jour qui

---

[5] Bouraoui suggests that the binary opposition between male and female (paradigmatic of other binary oppositions like nature/culture, childhood/adulthood, civilization/barbarism) has ended in our time. The traditional woman who remains at home and raises her children is rapidly becoming, or has become, a thing of the past. Alain Touraine quotes Lacan, contrasting the traditional view of man – « L'homme a le salut »– to that of woman – « La femme est le salut ». According to that view, both are subordinated to the phallic order, but that order has been overturned. Man no longer represents possession and reason, woman being and passion, for women (and many men) have disengaged themselves from that determinism, or binary opposition.

construisent la strophe d'un poème à jamais inachevé » (55). Samir alludes to Dumas, Laclos, Flaubert,[6] Boris Vian. It sounds as if the would-be poet, Samir, a latter-day Léon Dupuis if ever there was one, is looking at life through the filter of literature, instead of drawing upon life to create literature. As Flaubert remarked of Léon Dupuis, « Chaque petit notaire porte en lui les débris d'un poète ».

Héloïse speaks of Soufi music, « une sorte d'écriture invisible entre ciel et mer », a bridge Samir and Héloïse also try to create. The three friends and Héloïse dine at « La Calanque Blanche » – a « calanque » is a kind of boat, reinforcing the maritime imagery – a seafood restaurant, facing a glacial Mediterranean. Again, Samir fantasizes that she is the Belle of fairy tales: « Les trois mousquetaires et la Belle à la Mer Voyant » (59). Food imagery, like sea imagery, reinforces our sense of character. Héloïse orders an « île flottante » for dessert, symbolizing her fate on Djerba. After the *deux mousquetaires* leave, alone with Samir she becomes « une statue de marbre ». Samir wonders if she needs an audience to show love, if it is a performance, « sa *performance* amantine » (emphasis mine). Héloïse withdraws into her shell « une fois le message passé » (60).

There follow the two most important examples of Héloïse's own discourse, as the torch passes to her. One is visual, the fresco she has been commissioned to paint in the synagogue, whose Rabbi is a wealthy Tunisian. The second is verbal, the long letter in italics in which she explains her reasons for breaking off with Samir. In both cases, the apparently passive Muse, object of the gaze of others, strikes back – or faithful Penelope is transformed into a female Ulysses.

First, Héloïse takes Samir to the synagogue to view her fresco; it is a kind of test which he fails. We are reminded that in the synagogue women are separated from men by curtains (61), a cleavage true of Semitic societies in general. Héloïse lights up the place both physically and spiritually. As the fresco is described, « Héloïse donnait dans l'abstrait. Aucune représentation figurative » (62). This abstraction belongs to the Arabic tradition, with its non-representational art, its arabesques and stylized geometrical constructs. So just as she has tried to bring three religions to the table at « La Calanque Blanche », she tries to bring at least

---

[6] Héloïse remarks, like Madame Bovary, « La mer est belle, n'est-ce pas ? ». But Madame Bovary never gets to see the sea which so captivates her imagination.

two to the synagogue. The fresco has three levels: (1) « la vie quotidienne », daily life, (2) stars « couleur sable du désert », and (3) Genesis, a « souffle inaugural du *prosème* de l'univers » (62; emphasis mine). The fresco offers « Toute une Cosmogonie inspirée du Premier Livre de l'Ancien Testament ». The Book of Genesis appears in all three religions, and is here viewed as a prose poem. The birth of the world, of man, is also the birth of language: "In the beginning was the Word, and the Word was with God, and the Word was God". The Bible anticipates the Word Made Flesh (as *Ainsi Parle la Tour CN* ends with "the Word made Stone"). Héloïse seems to have chosen the abstract in place of the literally figurative, in the hope the viewer (in this case Samir) will be sufficiently engaged to complete the work: « Le figuratif est banni par une Genèse des traits et des couleurs qui ... enfante nos lucides consciences » (62). Even a « mandala bouddhique » (from the world of *Bangkok Blues*) is included, and the fresco takes advantage of the warm colors of the Mediterranean, where all three religions were born. Héloïse has painted « La Porte de Jérusalem » which does not seem to open, suggesting the political impasse in the region. In a synagogue she has even dared to use the colors of the dome of the mosque of Al-Aqsa.

Samir once again experiences vertigo at the « Envol d'Anges », « cet univers débordant d'espoir et de poèmes printaniers » (63), in contrast to wintry Marseille. The fresco visually illustrates Héloïse's quest for origins, including the birth of the human creative imagination. She quotes Ezekiel on "the grapes of wrath" (John Steinbeck's interpretation): « Les pères ont mangé les raisins verts et les dents des fils ont été agacés » (63). Samir thinks only that Héloïse may be alluding to suffering caused by her ancestors, a wound she has never managed to assuage. As usual, he misses the allusion to himself.

No wonder, then, that a disappointed, distracted Héloïse becomes lost in Marseille: « Elle se perd dans sa propre cité, ne retrouvant même pas l'artère principale » (64). She begins, moreover, to address Samir as « vous », thereby distancing him. His house of cards collapses because of the « vouvoiement », and because he realizes finally that Héloïse was never Jean-Marc's mistress, and that the latter lied to him. He finds himself « éjecté dans un univers incompréhensible », and the reader can only wonder why (64). Would he really prefer it had she been an old man's kept woman, rather than pure and chaste, and dealing only with « un père naturel »?[7]

There follow eight months of silence from Héloïse towards Samir, from December to July. In the ninth month she gives birth, but to a letter of rupture (or an abortion?). He has tried to call her three times, and again has occupied her room 305 at the Elmansiya, like a voyeur, only to discover she had checked out the day before.

The letter is her verbal form of expression following upon the fresco as her visual. There is a progression from abstract art to language. The epistolary form is very female, as women always excelled at writing letters and keeping journals. It is also courageous and confrontational. She accuses Samir of seeing her as « *Une détraquée !* » (66). She imagines him repeating this label a thousand and one times, day and night, evoking Scheherazade, the archetypal female artist. She knows that he sees her out of control, out of order, as even a Swiss bank or watch can be, a curious comparison calling up the clichéd image of the Swiss as neutral, passionless, misogynistic, materialistic[8]. She sets the rules, referring to « *notre première et unique rencontre* », indicating flatly that she has no intention of seeing him again (66).

She then proceeds to elaborate on her reasons for distancing herself. Of Tunisia, she says, « *...je suis faite d'une seule pièce. Pour moi, le retour au pays est une source intarissable de bonheur* » (as it is for Bouraoui himself and the characters of *Retour à Thyna*), while Samir has tried to deny his origins. She repeats to him the *dicton*, « *Fais-lui du couscous, il retrouvera ses origines* ». She continues by criticizing his two "buffers", the *deux mousquetaires*, and reveals what he has not suspected. André is no true artist because he did not accept her « *invitation au voyage* [echo of Baudelaire] *dans le royaume mystique des arts* », refusing to view her fresco (67). Mabrouk, to top it all off, played "footsies" with her under the table, and was « *plus donjuanesque que toi* ». Both of them tried to « *tirer les marrons du feu de la passion* ». Again, she

---

[7] I could not help thinking of Henry James's Frederick Winterbourne in *Daisy Miller* (1878), who is very ambivalent about Daisy. He cannot seem to make up his mind whether he would prefer her as a fallen woman, therefore accessible to his own lust, or a chaste young girl on the marriage market, whom he would have to court in due form.

[8] D. H. Lawrence comments on this notion of Swiss mind- and soul-numbing boredom in *Twilight in Italy* (1916).

repeats a proverb, defining his guilt by association: « *Dis-moi qui tu hantes et je te dirai qui tu es !* »

She is glad that Samir, at least, went to the synagogue with her, but he did not pass the test because he lacked her artistic spirit, and could not collaborate « *dans toute passion qui transfère beauté et vérité en Dieu vers l'homme* ». She seems to conjure up John Keats's "Beauty is truth, truth beauty", – that is all/Ye know on earth, and all ye need to know" – a religion of art that is totally beyond Samir, that would-be poet seduced by French literature, a literature not his own. Samir failed to participate in the movement from Chaos to Cosmos signified by the fresco, her composition. He has failed to compose, for one needs words, as God created the Word: « Mais un amour, aussi minime soit-il, peut-il être pris au sérieux s'il n' est pas mis en paroles... » (68). She admits that, with Jean-Marc, she was simply trapped in the spider web of origins. His supposed affair with her mother occurred with « *sa légitime épouse abandonnée à sa marmaille et mon père cloué à son commerce* » (68).

According to the letter, the old writer at the hotel Elmansiya fills in the gaps for Héloïse on her parentage, but is also playing his own game, and offers a paradoxical « *éclaircissement en clair-obscur* », which is a contradiction in terms. He calls her supposed parents « *un couple bizarre, mal assorti* », which, not coincidentally, is also the way Samir originally saw Jean-Marc and Héloïse. He uses a marine image to describe Marie the Corsican's mastery of the situation: « *Marie menait sa barque émotionnelle avec le doigté et la discrétion d'une véritable Djerbiya* » (70). He knows that gossip (comparing French and Tunisian) attributed two lovers to Marie, a French Catholic and an Arabo-musulman. As we have suspected for long enough, Ali Ben Mokhtar could equally be her father, especially if he is "the Chosen One".

Héloïse recounts how she met Jean-Marc just when she had lost all hope of motherhood, having been divorced for ten years. He was like the black tide, she says: « *La nature sait se venger des hommes qui l'ont saccagée* ». She attributes this phenomenon to Mektoub, or fate. She identifies a quasi-incestuous wish on the part of this « Don Juan décrépit », this « écrivain moribond »: « *...il s'est épris d'amour pour sa propre fille* » (71). She throws him out when he becomes too possessive, the only point of contact between their stories. She also reveals his racist attitude towards "Sam". In the final analysis, she feels certain that Jean-Marc was not really her natural father,[9] that he was merely using « *les ruses d'un renard roublard* », or, to mix metaphors, trying to keep his sinking ship afloat (72-3). He never took any interest in her art, because he was « *complètement enfermé en lui-même* » (73). Thus Samir becomes her sole hope of finding empathy, understanding: « *L'Inconnu, l'Étranger, le Nomade dans le pays de tes anciens colons* ». Thus she tries to identify with him, composing not only herself but Samir. She composed him « *de toutes pièces* » (as Francine does Barka's notes), while she is all of one piece (74). She admits she is « *une mer houleuse aux vagues chamarrées* », unlike her mother who navigated skillfully! She refuses to found a cult of Samir's personality, and concludes with a saying of the Tunisian St. Augustine: « *Donne de l'affection et fais ce que tu veux* » (75). Is she telling Samir to stop sitting on the fence, to commit, to take risks?

There are probably three more verbal compositions from her, the first, the mysterious prose poem from Stavanger Fjord in Norway (we don't know why her quest takes her there, except it is the extreme North, the polar opposite to Tunisia), in which she refers to Samir as « ô toi [*tutoiement* again], *le Composé* de terre, d'huile et de bouchées d'oublis ! » (92). Again, she seems to push him towards risk, towards commitment.

We learn as well that her quest incorporates an acquisition of language, even though in her letter she has said that « *l'écriture n'est pas mon genre. Mais j'aime la poésie comme les arts visuels* » (73). She learns not only Tunisian dialect, but « l'Arabe classique pour saisir les subtilités des versets coraniques » (92). Without language she cannot plant her roots. Not only does she construct her house at Chott El-Nador near Houmt-Souk, the largest city on Djerba – she is after all a trained architect – but she also decorates the interior, and increasingly turns to painting as her means of expression.

On Christmas Day, her birthday, she writes in her agenda of a dream in which Ali Ben Mokhtar appears as an unlikely St. Nicholas, and she awakens terrified after imagining herself in the arms of the wretched Mabrouk. After creating her ancestral home, « Le Heurte-Vent » [sounds like the French translation of Emily Brontë's *Wuthering Heights*, *Les Hauts de Hurle-Vent*], she has « Plus de nostalgie de la mer. Elle la contemple chaque matin dans une quiétude du bien vivre et du bien se sentir dans sa peau » (93). Evidently, she has found peace at last.

---

[9] Though the critic Nicola D'Ambrosio seems to accept that he is, and the whole matter is left ambiguous.

After the dream, her last *written* communication to Samir [beginning « *Cher Vous* »] is unsent. All of the letters are hers, in the female voice. She speaks of the limits of language, of the frustrated « *bonheur des mots* », yet of its necessity, of the constant tension between silence and language, quoting a famous writer: « *Tout ce qui est important doit rester discret, voire confidentiel. D'autre part, tout le monde a besoin de langue...* » (97). She compares identity, or one's "truth", to a faithful dog always following in your footsteps, and called "Love" (in English). She lives on silence and solitude, « *cette éternelle solitude* » (98). Her "maternal" instinct [does there not also exist a "paternal"?] is for continuation, duration: « *...la seule justification de la vie est de donner la vie, que notre raison d'exister réside fondamentalement dans la transmission. On ne peut exister sans vouloir durer...* » (99). Like Édith Piaf, she says, « Je ne regrette rien... », but she adds, « sauf la perte de mon enfant ... » (93). We never know if this is a child to her husband lost during her suicide attempt, or simply the child she has never had. It is difficult to see how to take this remark, because she is manifestly a woman who has not wanted to have a child by the wrong man – and she has never met the right one (although presumably when she was twenty her dashing husband may have seemed perfect). She does regret having produced only abstract art: « *Et toute la mère en moi pleure de ce grand devoir qu'elle éprouve de ne plus procréer que l'art abstrait* » (99). She is not satisfied with her means of continuation, and Samir never marries or commits. But she ends the unsent letter, « *Je demeure près de vous* », in spirit, presumably.

Héloïse is underestimating her achievement, does not realize that she has progressed beyond abstract art to language, and to painting that seems impressionistic, if not representational. Architecture itself, the first of her arts, breaks the usual feminine bounds of achievement, and has been recognized, by Emerson and Thoreau, among others, as second of the arts after literature, because it meets human needs, is functional and organic. As Bouraoui's description of her on the cover suggests, she has found a kind of serenity: « ...elle sortira armée d'une sérénité qui fera l'envie de tous »[10]. It seems that in a sense she and Samir have changed places. She no longer has a death wish, as her painting helps her to « voir clair... Elle

---

[10] Bouraoui has said that « Il faut composer avec la différence, avec l'altérité », which is exactly the lesson Héloïse has learned. The novel, and its heroine, find their resolution not in dogma, but in the artistic aspects of life. Héloïse, he adds, is going to emerge from her dilemma by means of a certain « repli sur soi ».

sait que l'art ne peut sauver la vie, mais qu'il peut accompagner les maladresses du vivre » (99). This is an existential resolution, at least, and one that is responsible for her last message to Samir, in the form of a painting not totally abstract that seems to suggest « un grand rond orange et jaune, un coucher de soleil, peut-être ». It reaches Samir, significantly, through his mother, a traditional woman who seems herself to be evolving. The signature, « Héla Ben Mokhtar », indicates that Héloïse has totally assimilated with her chosen land, the land of origin, and that Ali Ben Mokhtar is probably her real (or "Chosen"?) father. For Samir, on the other hand, the failed artist, the painting, transported back to Marseille, is his Black Box, reminding him forever of what *could* have been.

La femme d'entre les lignes

roman

Hédi Bouraoui

Éditions du Gref
Collection Le beau mentir

VI

The Man Behind *La Femme d'entre les lignes*

A sudden blow : the great wings beating still
Above the staggering girl, her thighs caressed
By the dark webs, her nape caught in his bill,
He holds her helpless breast upon his breast.

How can those terrified vague fingers push
The feathered glory from her loosening thighs?
And how can body, laid in that white rush,
But feel the strange heart beating where it lies?

A shudder in the loins engenders there
The broken wall, the burning roof and tower,
And Agamemnon dead.

Being so caught up,
So mastered by the brute blood of the air,
Did she put on his knowledge with his power,
Before the indifferent beak could let her drop?

(William Butler Yeats, 1923)

A terse little novel, like its predecessor *La Composée* (2001), *La Femme d'entre les lignes* (2002) yet leaves fewer handholds for the wary climber. Most critics seem determined to find the man behind the woman between the lines, but in the process they lose sight of the *aspect ludique*, the playfulness and irony. The reader seems to stick at each new twist of the plot.

The cover painting, by Lionel Tona, gestures at the Baroque, the Italian Renaissance. But, more importantly, its subject, the rape of Leda by Jupiter in the guise of a swan, suggests its reduplication in the text, and instantly brings to mind the most famous verbal version of "Leda and the Swan", that of William Butler Yeats. Leda is to be the mother of those dangerous twins, Helen, wife of King Menelaus, the beauty of the ancient world, whose supposed kidnapping, or seduction, by the Trojan Paris started the Trojan War, and Clytemnestra, who conspired with her lover Aegisthus at the murder of her husband Agamemnon. Another version of the story has Leda giving birth to twin boys, Castor and Polydeuces, the Dioscuri, but Yeats certainly highlighted the twin girls. Yeats asks the crucial question of Leda, as history has of her daughters:

> Being so caught up,
> So mastered by the brute blood of the air,
> Did she put on his knowledge with his power
> Before the indifferent beak could let her drop?

Bouraoui has thus evoked twinning, which can be viewed as replication in art. At the end he defines the *dédoublement* of his narrative voice: «Je viens donc de me détacher d'un moi pour narrer à la troisième personne, l'histoire de mon autre en moi qui est attelé au couple créé pour l'amour de percer l'énigme d'un *migramourir* à l'aube d'un siècle nouveau » (133). Art shares love's brutality, its violence and ruthlessness. In *Mensonge poétique et vérité romanesque*, René Girard proposes that it takes a third element, in the form of sexual jealousy, to create love. Bouraoui seems to have squared the equation, since each of the protagonists has a double.

The Book of the Swan is, in French, a pun, the Book of the Cygne/Signe. The Swan is Jupiter, the Father of us all, and Bouraoui explores the Oedipus Complex – or perhaps the Electra Complex – throughout the novel. Lisa, by abandoning him, metaphorically kills the father-figure the narrator has become to her, as Clytemnestra killed Agamemnon, and her sister Helen became "the face that launched a thousand ships", sending men to the Trojan War, a primordial setting for poets. As G. M. Kirkwood remarks, "The figures and stories concerned in it have provided material for poets, painters, playwrights, and sculptors from the time of Homer to the present moment" (99). The epic goes back to the "Egg" of Leda, "beginning *ab ovo*, from the egg" (Kirkwood 99). We are looking, then, at the gestation of art, at sexuality as a metaphor for the creative process. The narrator recognizes that « l'œuvre contient une partie de réflexion sur son proper processus créateur » (137). That it is metaphor, rather than life, is underlined by the fact that, in reality (*pace* Jupiter), swans are not promiscuous, mate for life, and die when their mate dies.

Bouraoui's novel reflects this permeable bipolarity of art and life. The first part, « Parchemin de la Mémoire », seems realistic : it gives the family background of both principals, Marguarita Felice/aka Lisa, and the unnamed male narrator. The second part, on the other hand, « Migramour », veers towards Symbolism, perhaps even allegory. Lisa is presented as "real", as we are enticed into the requisite "suspension of disbelief" in Part One, whereas Palimpseste is "created" (the narrator's creation), like Virebaroud, Lisa's creation, and these two fictive characters take over at the end of the novel.

Part One, « Parchemin de la Mémoire », and Part Two, « Migramour », are themselves already twinned, as mirror images of the so-called "real" and "fictive". « Lisa s'éclipse » partway through « Migramour ». As a reader she lives only for and in the narrator's work, and later, fittingly, becomes a fictional character. At first she is in the position of ideal reader, perhaps critic – though the latter possibility is undermined by her apparent lack of critical sense or judgment, her contribution to his work being essentially that of a conscientious proofreader and editor of his style and language. By Part Two Lisa becomes Palimpseste, the narrator's fictional creation. But by the end, the tables are turned, and Virebaroud becomes *her* fictional creation (but again not original, and derived from traits of heroes he has created in his novels). The name "Vire/baroud" suggests the Latin "vir", man, and "baroud" would mean a man in conflict, in battle, like the heroes of the Trojan War. It may also echo Virgulius, the protagonist of *Bangkok Blues*, Bouraoui's earlier novel, whose name also evoked Virgil, creator of the epic poem about the founding of Rome in the aftermath of the Trojan War, the Aeneid. Towards the end of the novel we also meet a failed (but popular), comical poet named Virgilio Scapin, whose last name suggests Molière's comic rogue in *Les Fourberies de Scapin*.

Bouraoui's first title, *Migramour*, now the title of the second part, also calls up the wanderings of warriors, including Odysseus and Aeneas, during the Trojan War, and the eventual founding of Rome, Italy being his chosen setting for this novel.

We encounter both male twins, the narrator and Virebaroud, Lisa's name for him, as well as Lisa herself who disappears abruptly / metamorphoses into Palimpseste. Palimpseste, presumably, has had many texts written upon her. Is she all women in one, as Virebaroud is all men in one? Or a work in progress, perhaps *le livre absolu* the narrator dreams of? Elizabeth Ermarth has said that Identity "is in processes. It is in a state of 'palimpsestuousness' [a term borrowed from Michael Alexander]" (412) – perhaps implying incest as well: which is the creator, which the creation?

The final title chosen, however, is more nuanced, sexier, if you will, because it puns; it can be the woman between the lines of paper, or between the « draps », the sheets.

I. « Le Parchemin de la Mémoire » : The Encounter

The first part is the shortest of the novel, but the narrator is immediately introduced as a poet, as his writing material, « par/chemin », could be translated as "the road of memory", the product of wanderings, as well as the product on which he writes. The "road" motif creates a parallel with « Migr/a/mour ». « Migr/a/mourir » is also implied, but by omitting the final « ir » Bouraoui suggests the triumph of love/art over death. Love itself becomes *more* real in its artistic expression, is carried to another level in which memory, or re-creation, triumphs over a somewhat banal reality. The titles of both parts convey the sense that this is a journey or quest novel, modeled on epic poems, the Iliad, the Odyssey, the Aeneid. The narrator calls himself « L'Errant », the Wanderer (title of an Old English poem, as well as the English translation of Alain-Fournier's 1913 novel (in French *Le Grand Meaulnes*), on which Bouraoui began his early scholarship. But « L'Errant » could also be the Mistaken One, he who "errs", or wanders astray. It is left to the reader to resolve the ambiguity if s/he can.

La Femme d'entre les lignes is, in the final analysis, a book about art, and the love of art. Only in that sense is it a love story. In any fictional account of the gestation of the novel as genre, gender plays a part: we have "mothers of the novel" and "fathers of the novel" – mothers and fathers, parents against whom one rebels but whose influence remains strong, loom large in this work.

We find ourselves, in Part One, in medias res on a cross-cultural note. The « Je » is not identified, but he finds himself in a cold country with "a thick layer of ice buried under fresh snow" (9). But the first place actually mentioned is Verona, in a warm Mediterranean land, where, we learn later, Lisa was born, « loin, très loin dans ce pays du soleil, si different de celui de mon enfance, et pourtant si semblable » (9). His "burning desire" clashes sharply with the ice and snow. In a metaphor for perception he must clear his car windshield of ice, « pour voir clair dans les images embrouillées de mon esprit fatigué » (9). What is fatiguing, in fact, is his *imaginaire.* One thinks of Willa Cather's stated desire "to freeze the world in the grip of form". But there is both stasis and movement here, like the Buddhist wheel. « Loin » and « lointain » are constantly repeated like a mantra – far from the one he loves, perhaps, but far by choice, firing the imagination and the road of memory.

When these two would-be lovers meet, he who writes compulsively, and she who has devoured his books for ten years without knowing him, the scene has comic overtones, for they can converse fumblingly only in English, which is equally foreign to both. This is a book about language, but also about blocked communication: « Il [English] ne traduit pas au cheveu près ce qui se trouve à l'intérieur de nous » (13). Nor does he hesitate to mock the hegemony of English, « cette maudite langue qui fait frissonner le monde entier » (one thinks of the fractured, possibly dyslexic language of George W. Bush).

There is even instant conflict between these two, from southern Europe and North Africa. She tosses his stuffed dates, prepared with loving care by his sister, in her handbag. They are joined by the Mediterranean, but also separated by it: « Mais ne suis-je pas plus sudiste qu'elle ? » (15). He has, moreover, roots in three diametrically opposed places: « Et moi dont le sud va plus loin que les confins de son Italie méridionale, jusqu'à la terre africaine d'où il a été ballotté, jusqu'au nord le plus nordique des arpents de neige, de glas, et de verglas ! » (16).

His friend Roberto shows a portrait of his children that, to the narrator's eyes, looks like a valentine inspired by Lisa. But Roberto also indulges in a philosophic discussion about the link between love and politics: « ... on est toujours rongé par son proper intérêt » even when it is an *égoïsme à deux.* The narrator tries to feel without phrases or metaphors: « C'est la rencontre fortuite qui déclenche en nous les plus sublimes amours... » (17). Later, however, he is to admit that he has to *write* it in order to feel pain: « Il m'a fallu écrire la disparition de Lisa pour me rendre compte de l'effet à la fois dévastateur et bénéfique d'une telle épreuve » (131).

Suddenly we are transported to Québec Air, and to another woman reminiscent of Lisa (aren't they all?). *Québécoise* that she is, however, she looks more Italian than Lisa. He imagines himself making love to her "with *silent* words" (emphasis mine), and finds being called a poet "monstrously pompous" (22). Yet he is word-obsessed: there are the constant echoes of Baudelaire – « mes forêts de symboles » (23), of Laclos – « ... cette liaison qui, loin d'être dangereuse, n'en demeure pas moins exceptionnelle » (23). He boasts, « Nous sommes, en avion archiplein, le seul couple à faire l'amour en privé » (21). He enjoys an unspoken/unpublished ? « jouissance charnelle inédite » (22) with his brunette, as Lisa is blonde: « Blonde Lisa n'a d'italien que l'amplification des gestes » (19).

He imagines Lisa slipping between the sheets, « pour bien être dans tes pages » (22). He seems mainly concerned with choosing « les mots justes », words to capture her essence. The reader is often tempted to say to her, "Get a life", but we soon learn she has one – an aged mother stricken with Alzheimer's who never lets her out of her sight. He understands because his mother, even when young and healthy, also clung tenderly to him, even though he was for the most part in distant lands. Lisa takes the male role, ordering for him in the restaurant where they begin their flesh-and-blood acquaintance. She hangs on his every word, his ideal audience, and he wonders how to satisfy her, for he may give her poison instead of elixir (25). She is also jealous of his reading public, and she seeks to swallow him up: « Je disparus en elle! Mon sexe vogue dans sa lune en feu d'un soleil couchant » (27). Is he the sun god (« couchant », sleeping with her), she the moon goddess?

There are subtle hints from the start that all is not well with this relationship, that each is trying to create the other in his/her own image. Even her name, Lisa, is his creation, perhaps for Élisabeth, which means "dedicated to God». One cannot resist asking if he, the artist, considers himself a God of creation (like Jupiter). Her real name, Marguarita Felice, translates as the marguerite, or daisy, a flower sacred to the Court of Love tradition, a symbol which still survives today in the form of plucking its petals to discover true love. In case we miss the reference, the lines pass through the narrator's mind: « *Je t'aime un peu, beaucoup, passionnément, pas du tout…* » (10). Her last name, "Felice", or happiness, may be valorized by the consummation of their love in erotic, yet verbal rather than animalistic, terms. It may also be ironic in that his true happiness resides in memory. One thinks of Flaubert's hero Frédéric Moreau in *L'Éducation sentimentale* who avers that the best experience he ever had was turning away on the steps of a bordello, and therefore never soiling the dream of love. The narrator speaks of the climax of their lovemaking as a « Plénitude inattendue », but the very Derridean frame of reference underlines that this is not copulation, but a « double promenade dans notre imaginaire » (27). We wonder, is any of this really happening?

She hangs breathlessly on his every word as he describes his literary award of the Fleur de Lys in his own province, « la Fleur de Lys, ce célèbre symbole de la province francophone que j'ai effeuillé en triade identitaire: Nord-Américains, Européens, Africains » (28). This man of three continents (like his creator Hédi Bouraoui) learns, as Lisa says, that it is always a pleasure to be recognized in one's own province and country. It was Virgil who wrote, not of his epic the Aeneid, but of the Georgics, his book about farming near the Mincio where he was born, "For I shall be the first, if I live, to bring the Muse into my own country", or *patria*, meaning not Rome, or even Italy, but "the little rural neighbourhood on the Mincio where the poet was born" (Cather 171).[1]

The narrator feels a conflict between Lisa's recognition of his art, and pleasure at his prize, and her bitterness at having been excluded from the event. He wonders if he has missed the time for her to open herself to his most burning words, and he describes how he might have mistreated, misshaped her, borrowing the words of a critical establishment he despises: « Je l'aurais défaite, déformée comme un critique qui dissèque un corps-texte de mots empruntés, de panoplies d'acrobaties linguistiques, de subterfuges stylistiques » (28).

Does Lisa really read him « entre les lignes »? (88). Or does he read her? He expresses admiration for her impressionistic, subjective criticism, and hatred for academic critics: « ... tu ne lis pas mes vers comme un critique *savant* qui applique stupidement une certaine grille méthodologique, mais pour extraire *l'essence de l'œuvre*, tu lis ma poésie avec le cœur : car l'amour qui s'appropie les amours de l'autre et les fait siennes... C'est ça l'Amour ! Quel plaisir ! » (50). The phrasing makes us suspicious about both of them, but not in the sense Didier Leclair suggests when he summarizes his reaction:

---

[1] Willa Cather has one of her characters in *My Antonia* (1918), Gaston Cleric, Jim Burden's teacher, quote Virgil to this effect: *"Primus ego in patriam mecum ... deducam Musas"*, Cather's own *patria* being the Nebraska prairies where she was raised from the age of ten, and *My Antonia* being her modernist version of the Georgics.

« Ce livre m'a plu. Il vous enseignera que badiner avec l'amour, ce n'est pas aimer. Même si un poète tente de vous prouver le contraire » (68)[2]. Leclair ignores the deliberate ironic deflation of the narrative voice, who is to be displaced in any event by the end of the novel.

We are never given any concrete examples of her critical perspicacity. She writes brief book reviews for an Italian newspaper, *La Repubblica.* One wonders if they really capture « la substantifique moelle de mon écriture » (96), or, indeed, if there is any « substantifique moelle » to begin with. In a reversal of the biological order, it is he who gives birth – to poetry, or the Word made Flesh. Her contributions seem to be fairly minor: « Dès que le corps-texte sort de mes entrailles, elle se met à chasser les coquilles ; javelliser les anglicismes, mailloter les dérives... Mais elle n'ose jamais toucher à mes africanismes du Nord ou ceux du sud du Sahara » (127). Indeed, we can only guess what she is correcting, if their only common languages are Italian and English !Metaphorically speaking, she seems to be washing the diapers!

Lisa, we learn later, aspires herself to be a creative writer. One wonders if her final withdrawal signals an increase in self-confidence, the adoption of a writing career. The narrator speculates that she has become a Judas, betraying him (or his ego?). Certainly Palimpseste, « l'autre vérité de Lisa » (141), takes over all the correspondence at the end of the novel, and the "narrator" himself withdraws, as the novel moves to third person, and to the epistolary form which marked the very beginnings of the novel in the seventeenth and eighteenth centuries. The epistolary novel was the subgenre that proved empowering both to women writers and to heroines created by male authors, such as Richardson's Pamela (174) and Clarissa (1749) in England, Marivaux's Marianne in *La Vie de Marianne* (1731-41), and Laclos' Madame de Merteuil in *Les Liaisons dangereuses* (1782) in France. Lisa and the narrator first meet through a ten-year correspondence, evoking

---

[2] Leclair seems to blur the distinction between author and fictional creation: « Sa liberté est toute personnelle... Ce libertin jouit, sans plus. Si l'amante y trouve son compte, tant mieux. Du moment que Lisa se pâme devant ses textes et (peut-être) dans son lit, il y a eu échange de bons procédés amoureux. Mais est-ce cela, l'amour ?... Lisa n'a droit qu'à sa fougue de coq insatiable du mot et à la version subjective de sa rupture avec Rose » (68). If Leclair only hints at an autobiographical reading, Mireille Desjarlais-Heynneman has no such reservations and traces point by point the correlation of author and protagonist, thereby missing all the irony.

Baudelaire's fusion of the senses in « Correspondances »: « Les mots, les couleurs et les sons se répondent ». The narrator writes of this « forme de correspondance soutenue qui a établi entre nous une fidélité matrimoniale sans acte de mariage... » (93). We wonder if Lisa moves finally from Muse/Qasîd (poem) to poet, and in fact reverses the narrator's expectations by inventing him, thereby becoming not only the twin of Palimpseste, but that of the narrator/Virebaroud.[3]

This eventual role reversal is foreshadowed in Part One by the umbrella Lisa carries to their meeting at a café-bistro: he begins to think that this "phallic" object represents « la tierce personne du triangle eternal des amoureux » (46), whom Girard sees as the spur to love. To the protagonist, it seems for a time a weapon , similar to the famous Bulgarian umbrella which allowed a spy from the Eastern Bloc to kill an important personage in the middle of London during the Cold War between the Americans and the Communists (48). It reinforces his sense of her occasionally adopting the male, aggressive role, in that he associates her with an assassin. But she freely offers him shelter under it, *« Un p'tit coin d'parapluie »* (53).

The equation of love, violence, and death has already been planted in the narrator's mind by a parallel love/hate story to their own within Lisa's family, that of her beloved niece Anna and the unemployed would-be artist, the Moroccan Ali who also, not coincidentally, works on parchment, but badly, practicing his crude art that no one wants to exhibit, or even to buy (31). These two are descending to the last circle of a Dantesque hell – will Lisa and the narrator escape their fate?

During their walk by the sea, Lisa and the narrator exchange sexual/gender identity: « ... nous avons changé nos corps. Le mien transsexue en elle. Le sien transsexue en moi » (38) ; thus they are twinned. But it is clear that this love is composed more of words than of physicality, « de mots qui font le sens de ce que nous sommes" (38).

Their dialogue always focuses on his art, not on the mutual sharing of a love relationship. We wonder whether she is overestimating him. She knows, rightly, that he is not a romantic poet: « Tu ne vas pas dans l'au-delà pour ramener des visions extraordinaires au commun des mortels » (47). She sees his thematic originality as the destruction of the traditional couple,

[3] Éric Gauthier assumes that the narrator is Virebaroud, « un poète maghrébin habitant au Québec » (27), but in fact it is the collective name Lisa/Palimpseste attaches to all his heroes.

providing a new way to love, to make love, and to speak about it (48) – but again, we are given no examples in his writing (or indeed of his writing) apart from this book in the form of a memoir.

He seems obsessed with the idea that she has had earlier lovers, that he does not possess her utterly. But he himself has had one noteworthy mistress, and this affair becomes a tale within a tale, which casts doubt on his supposedly new constitution of the couple. The mistress's name is Rose, a symbolic name attached to the Virgin, and therefore a flower appropriated by the secular Court of Love Tradition based on Marian Worship. The Rose, according to the Court of Love, is a symbol of virginity in an enclosed garden, the *hortus clusus*, to be attained by the lover. Most importantly to Bouraoui, Rose is the desert rose, the « Rose des Sables », blooming fresh and pure in the midst of arid sands. The narrator's recounting of this sad affair ironizes him totally. This supposedly free-spirited poet has made a living – because « la poésie ne nourrit personne » (50) – selling the notoriously unpoetic, information-packed (and English) Encyclopedia Britannica [British], which aspires to universal *objective* knowledge. He thinks he is appeasing Lisa when he asserts that « celle que j'ai aimée te ressemble beaucoup... Je suis convaincu que nous tombons toujours amoureux du même type de femme ou d'homme » (51) – surely a misstep and a warning, implying that any woman of a single "type" has appealed, and will continue to appeal, to him. The only difference he sees is that Rose had chestnut (reddish) hair, and a voluptuous figure, while Lisa is blonde and (presumably) slim. Intelligent, sensitive, and a voracious reader, Rose was director of a large bookstore/publishing house (51). Her sole defect was that she could not tolerate his continual absences, and saw him as a tomcat: « ... j'étais toujours parti, comme un chat de gouttière aux moments où elle avait le plus besoin de moi » (51). Most readers would perceive Rose as likeable, arguably much more so than the mercurial Lisa, who seems to be a literary "groupie". But the narrator calls Rose's recriminations "unjustified" and self-righteously claims that « Je l'avertissais de l'imminente catastrophe où elle nous menait » (52). But it takes two to create a catastrophe in a love relationship, and he seems to disclaim all personal responsibility. He complains that « Elle n'a jamais accepté les règles du jeu » despite knowing them in advance, and that his work required frequent departures and long absences (52). These are scarcely the « règles du jeu » of an egalitarian, poetic, free love relationship. Moreover, his absences are not in aid of poetic expression, but of the mundane selling of the Encyclopedia Britannica.

It would be easy to assume (as Leclair and Desjarlais-Heynneman seem to) that author and narrator are one, but this tale can also be read as an exercise in unconscious self-revelation on the part of the narrator, who is subtly undermined by his creator, and finally displaced. We do not learn Lisa's reaction to this tale, except in her subsequent act of withdrawal; she may have identified all too closely with Rose. The narrative technique leaves it to the reader (and Lisa) to piece together the clues, fill in the gaps.

Lisa's religious background is also given at the end of the first part, but the information leads from the personal to an expansion into comparative religions and the overweening theme of tolerance. Lisa is a nominal Catholic, and the narrator evidently comes from an Islamic background. But the most attention is paid to his remembered Seder supper with the Eisens during the Jewish Passover. While on one level this minutely detailed account seems intrusive in the narrative, it opens it out from the rather claustrophobic "smother-love" story. This love affair – imaginary or "real" – becomes a paradigm for global, universal communion. The lamb is not a blood sacrifice, as it is in traditional monotheisms; rather, it is sacrificed on the altar of love, « Un amour qui unit » (64). Love itself thus becomes a religion, signifying an escape from the ego: « ... nous nous essayons à tuer la partie nombriliste de nous-mêmes afin que nos corps-textes prennent la revanche sur nos corps tout court! » (64).

Part One ends, however, not with the lamb of peace and eternal life, but with the tale of the cat trying to trap a mouse by barking like a dog to reassure its intended victim. Licking its chops, the cat says, « Voilà ce que c'est que d'être bilingue! » (65). This tale/tail (?) leads to the cat-and-mouse game of both lovers in Part Two, « Migramour ». Moreover, it suggests that Lisa may be transmogrifying into Rose, the first to call the narrator an alley cat.

II. « Migramour » : Love, Death, and Words

« Migramour » permits puns in French which simply do not work in English: a/mour/mour/ir/mort/maux/mots. Both parts begin and end with language. The narrator, like Dante at thirty-five, is "midway the journey of this life" and descends into an Inferno of his own making. He first perceives Lisa as his guide, therefore his Virgil, this despite the fact that she comes to see him as *Virebaroud*, whose name also suggests Virgil (as does Virgilio Scapin).

The title of this part ostensibly comes from a boat Lisa sometimes takes, *Le Migramour de Troie*, underlining the Trojan framework "palimpsestuously" inscribed on the parchment of memory beneath the present tense of the tale. The reference to the Mediterranean Sea, ancient and modern, is prefigured by the lovers' earlier walk by the sea. The sea also evokes the mother, symbolically in both French and English, but linguistically as well in French, as « mer » and « mère » are homonyms. Expanding the water imagery, the narrator calls his poems "a river where Lisa slakes her thirst" (71). Ironically, she gathers « les roses de sable aux petales intrigants", calling up memories of her predecessor Rose.

It is significant that the role of the mother is highlighted in this section. There is first a reference to an older woman friend, Anita, with whom he had a fraternal relationship; when she dies, he feels as if a part of his being had been amputated (78). Anita, and the flagrantly unpoetic Claudette Charbonneau, a radio interviewer, are two more of the women who appear on his palimpsestuous parchment of memory.

Groping in the darkness of memory, he visits the land of his birth, and returns to origins in the person of his mother Ibtisem (« Sourire ») (82). She does not pose a threat, unlike Lisa's mother. Proud of her son's authorship, she organizes a party in his honor, as a North African mother who rules not only her family, but also the world surrounding her. She displays his latest book on a table, but no one opens it, and the conversation turns on the weather, the plague of scorpions, the future of a young woman following her baccalaureate: « La soirée se passa sans qu'aucun mot n'ait été dit, ni du livre, ni de la musique » (Ibtisem hired a lute player). Ibtisem's comment is: « ... que l'on ne peut amener les brebis galeuses brouter une herbe autre hors des champs pollués de l'amour de soi ! » (82). His book took its title from the Du Bellay poem, but feminized : *« Heureuse qui comme la Mère a fait un beau voyage »* (83). But his mother travels by never leaving home, and she is never more present to her wandering son than during his absences. The mother, moreover, is substituted in the title for Ulysses in the poem, the archetypal quest hero/wanderer – though it is the narrator who wanders, and frequently wanders astray. When he goes back to Africa, back to Canada, Lisa, too, is more present to him in her absence: « L'absence de Lisa n'arrête pas de me séduire ... , elle plonge dans mes écrits » (63). The mother, and Lisa (at least for a time) play the role of faithful Penelope awaiting the return of Ulysses, following him only in their imaginations. The narrator parallels his work as a writer and Lisa's as a reader, her « lecture amantine » (81). Not only does she follow « les chemins [parchemin?] tortueux de mes écrits », but she is « en quête d'une vision initiatique... » (81). But will it be a female quest, a female initiation ?

Except for the subtitles, « Parchemin de la Mémoire » and « Migramour, » the words that appear most often in the text are « loin » and « lointain ». It seems clear that the narrator actually prefers absence to presence, so that he can re-create love of mother, of mistress(es) in his *« imaginaire »*. (The bordello you never enter is better than the one you do). There is an « amour nomade » (69), his art « une migration vibrante » (70). Their correspondence is « une bouteille jetée à la mer » (98), and Lisa's absence, if anything, inspires his art.

In « Migramour, » the *imaginaire* eventually takes over completely, as was predicted earlier in the narrator's reference to the dichotomy of art and life: « ... entre l'écrit et le vécu, il y a des espaces infinis qui m'effraient », a paraphrase of Pascal's « Le silence des espaces infinis m'effraie ». Pascal is talking about silence (God's), the narrator about words.

From time to time he begins to suspect that the "real" Lisa may be very different from the one he creates in his mind: « Je continue à la façonner à ma guise, à l'image que je me fais d'elle » (89). She becomes, in fact, his creation, Palimpseste. But he also begins to speculate whether she is creating him: « N'est-ce pas qu'à son tour elle me crée, elle-même de mes propres mots... » (89). As I have described elsewhere, often in Bouraoui's texts "The Muse Strikes Back", assumes herself the role of poet or artist. The narrator notes that the constant interchange between lived experience and its artistic recreation is analogous to sexual exchange: « ... il existe et existera toujours un décalage croissant entre l'expérience vécue et la transcription, entre la parole *parfaite* ... et les *chemins* tortueux, labyrinthiques, qu'elle doit suivre... » (95; emphasis mine).

From time to time, it occurs to the narrator to wonder if Lisa is in love with him, or with his writing (which she knew long before she met the author): « Cette demande d'amour, est-elle pour mes mots ou pour ma personne? » (61). At the end, he comments with some degree of bitterness, « Lisa me bannit de son cercle de lecture. Je me demande si elle m'aime pour moi-même ou pour mes écrits, pour la lutte que je mène avec les mots ou pour la trophée des jours de gloire, pour l'étincelle de vérité dans les silences entre les lignes ou pour la voix solitaire en incessantes demandes d'amour ? » (140). But she herself invents Virebaroud in the first sample we have of her own writing, the letter sent to North Africa (the « bouteille jetée de l'autre côté de la Méditerranée »): « Séduite par le pouvoir des mots, je suis tentée de voguer à ma guise, recréant le héros que je nomme Virebaroud, et qui incarne la synthèse de tous ses personnages » (103). Her creativity could be viewed as essentially false, however, or at least at a second remove, governed and inspired solely by his text(s). She paraphrases Pascal's « Le cœur a ses raisons que la raison ne connaît pas » when she claims that « Mon cœur suit ses inclinations même s'il ne les comprend pas » (104). But Pascal is talking about faith, Lisa about her supposed "love" for this « personnage fictif et reel à la fois » (104). In effect, she sees herself as an infant born from *his* labors: « ... je nais tour à tour de mes lectures, ... à la manière d'une fille qui fait naître sa mère en même temps que cette dernière la met au monde » (103). We have already learned that Lisa's mother, unlike Ibtisem, suffers from Alzheimer's, and that Lisa, as caregiver, is virtually a prisoner in her own home. She may aspire to be herself the mother of the text, as the narrator is the father. A weak mother rules her, while a strong mother supported the narrator.

Lisa, perhaps thinking of Rose, is a stern judge of feminine love:

> *Tout le dilemme est là : les femmes adorent se perdre dans l'homme, et une fois qu'elles l'ont trouvé, elles s'échinent à ne plus le lâcher. Paradoxe, diras-tu ? Et l'amour ne vit-il pas d'ambiguïté et de malentendu ? Et ne meurt-il pas par excès de lucidité ou de clairvoyance ?* (101)

This is a self-fulfilling prophecy, as she seems to become possessive, herself creating the creation, addressing him as « toi *mon* écrivain » (104; emphasis mine).

The text is replete with allusions to great lovers of the past, real and fictive – Romeo and Juliet, the triangle of Aïda, Radames, Amneris, and the negative role of the patriarchy which tries to destroy such relationships. The tragedy of the House of Atreus lurks "palimpsestuously" behind the tangled relations of the present.

Lisa is also compared to Bellini's portrait of the Madonna and Child, which is, not coincidentally, a triptych, with monks (or Fathers of the Church) depicted on the surrounding two panels. The narrator, revealingly, falls in love with this image not only for her divine beauty and perfection, but for the four readers surrounding her. In the right-hand panel, one monk holds a closed book, while the others are engaged in communal reading. In the left-hand panel, one monk faces the viewers, and holds an open book in his left hand: « Quelle belle invitation à la lecture! » comments our ever-avid author. The literal books reflect the Being the Madonna holds, who is the Word made Flesh. And we return to the concept of art as religion encountered first in Part One. As the narrator comments of the characters in the triptych, « Le Livre est au Cœur de leur vie. C'est du Livre que partent et reviennent les destins après les périples et les pérégrinations, les aventures et les sédentarismes, tous vécus entre les lignes » (110). A few pages later, however, an inscription on a Gothic Venetian house reminds him, "There are no Roses without thorns" (114) – and the Virgin's emblem is the Rose, also the name of his earlier love.

On his return from Africa, he expects to find Lisa reading him « à cœur ouvert » (106). But she has offered hints of her coming defection in the letter where she claims, « ... je sais tout de l'écrivain qui se cache derrière ces femmes qui peuplent son monde » (102). She seems to prefer the palimpsest of his work to that of his tangled life.

Palimpseste the female character is first introduced by name on page 87 by Pia (who is anything but pious), Lisa's drunken friend who momentarily sees herself as Beatrice to the narrator's Dante: « Tu n'es pas Dante, mais je t'adore ». Suddenly, the narrator finds himself confronted with Palimpseste, « Lisa ou plutôt l'Image-Lisa », as the "real" Lisa becomes the fictional Palimpseste. It is Pia who leaves a phone message on behalf of Palimpseste, requesting his phone number.

While Lisa is a journalistic critic who works with words, Palimpseste, as her name suggests, is an artisan who makes books physically, « tout le côté artisanal »: « ... j'aime le livre bien fait » (120). His relationship with her begins when, on page 120, « Lisa s'éclipse ». Between the two women, he has his ideal critic, and his means of production. We slowly begin to glean the motivation behind Lisa's disappearance. The narrator, as Palimpseste notes, creates an equation between art and love. Their boundaries disappear, and he stresses that only they will save us from the apocalypse. Lisa has said he is not a romantic poet, but he echoes Keats when he says that only « l'amour du beau, ou la beauté de l'amour » can save us. He wants to create « le livre absolu » (123). His liaison with Lisa – for he identifies her with her country – is a symbolic union of the ancient enemies Carthage and Rome.

If we are curious about what happens to the old Lisa in this new relationship, she breathes, « Je t'ai créé ... des limbes de mes mots » (123). Virebaroud, the male, promptly responds with sexual violence, « la poignarde de son arbitraire, et la dépossède violemment de toutes ses clefs de lecture » (123). She wants to die « dans les feuillages des chants du cygne [signe] », but the swan only sings when dying, in order to follow his/her mate. Lisa, who wants to write her own story, would have to kill him, like Clytemnestra, to survive herself, become the swan: « Pour ce faire, il lui faut tuer Virebaroud, s'en débarrasser en l'étouffant de baisers, en lui avalant sa langue pour lui ôter, une fois pour toutes, la voix » (124). Or she would have to betray him, like Helen. And indeed he accuses her of the latter, with a character of her own creation, but constructed out of his own fictional protagonists: « Et avec qui me trahit-elle ?Avec un personnage qu'elle a créé de toutes pièces » (135).

In the closing pages, he too transfers to Virebaroud, and is no longer the narrator, but a character in a third-person narration (133). The cosmos is perceived as « Mère universelle » (134), but the fathers will either kill or be killed, as Amonasro asks his daughter Aïda to betray her lover Radames to save her own country from the Egyptians. Aïda exclaims, «Ô patrie, combien tu me coûtes ! » (136). And the narrator asks, « Et Lisa, que trahit-elle ? » The answer is, « L'auteur qui a inspiré son amour ... et encore avec un homme de papier, un personnage tiré des vertèbres du poète ... ce n'est pas une trahison, mais un transfert » (136). As Palimpseste says, Lisa « tue le père qui féconde ses fantasmes, comme tu le fais, toi, avec les figures du père dans tes écrits » (137). And Palimpseste's response is that «comme toi, elle tue le père du livre, puis elle le ressuscite en Virebaroud... » (137). [The dead, or dying, father, or patriarch, also goes back to the murdered Agamemnon, and to Anchises, Aeneas's father, who perish in the classical epics]. Lisa, as a journalistic critic, says he, was at first distanced from the work, gathering a rose here, a daisy there. But she wanted more: « ... elle ne se contente pas de ce rôle de critique ; plutôt elle décide de s'attacher au personnage pour *migramourir* ... plus librement avec lui. Au fait, elle se débarrasse ainsi de l'auteur, et s'y substituant, elle devient, elle-même, l'auteur » (137). But the consequences are far more ambiguous than in Bouraoui's other novels where "The Muse Strikes Back". The novel grows out of love, death: « ... il faut bien détruire, pour reconstruire » (139). The narrator wonders if his mistake was to set the inner life in *real* time. The judge San Antonio (cartoon character? the businessman in *The Merchant of Venice?)* thinks that the narrator should have remained in the *oral* tradition from which he comes, not expose their relationship in written form.

The novel ends, however, with written words, in the form of correspondence between the two fictive characters, Palimpseste and Virebaroud. Their geographical distance is emphasized. The narrator feels at home in Toronto, « *le carrefour du monde* » (146), with all its faults of materialism: « *Tout est neuf et sans histoire* », « *tout le monde est immigré* », and he enjoys « *les feuilles mortes de l'été indien* » (150). [The description simply does not fit Montréal, though he seems to indicate earlier that his home is « La Belle ... Province ».] The ending thus resembles that of *La Composée*, though hero and heroine have equally the right to speak, whereas in the preceding novel Héloïse, in her final letter, undermines all of the hero's prior assumptions. Palimpseste is now not only producing, but distributing his books, again from a distance.

The novel, typically, ends with a P. S. on art, referring to the « *poème inachevé que j'ai du mal à parfaire* », which she is helping him to see clearly. And finally, the last word is a P. P. S. moving from art to life, from the personal to the universal. Virebaroud quotes a friend who declared that the greatest tragedy of the twentieth century is the systematic uprooting of people, leaving everything behind them – « *des mémoires saccagées, des tonnes de sentiments bafoués, violés, des charniers par milliers! Et des mots!* » (152).

Thus the novel ends, as it began, with words, and the pun on *maux/mots* is intentional, and was foreshadowed. Significantly, also, the ending leaves us with neither *amour* nor *mort*, but with *mots*, words, our only weapon against the darkness, a weapon which, as Sartre's *Les Mots* reminds us, must further existential *engagement*, commitment, eschew the merely lyrical as long as there is a child starving in the world. The novel thus denounces its own fictivity, but by the same token celebrates it. I was tempted to call this essay "The Man Behind the Man Behind *La Femme d'entre les lignes*" in order to draw a clear line of demarcation between creator and protagonist/artist, a line crossed by many critics. If fiction grows out of "lived experience", as Henry James put it, it is nevertheless distanced, often ironized, by form and art. James was careful to define experience as "impression", "the very air we breathe" (13). He adds to his hypothetical advice to a novice, "Write from experience and experience only", the crucial refinement, "Try to be one of the people on whom nothing is lost!" (13). Or, as critic R. P. Blackmur once wrote,

"Art is life at the remove of form and meaning". *La Femme d'entre les lignes* constitutes a reflection on art, denounces and at the same time celebrates its own fictivity by framing its love story in a postmodern world in quest of order while coping with chaos, like the ancient Greeks, Trojans, Romans, and Carthaginians.

CONCLUSION

Hédi Bouraoui's flight around the globe is coming in for a landing – if only a temporary one. Like Virgulius's and unlike Samir's, Bouraoui's does not "crash and burn", but carries hope for the future of the "global village", a hope articulated by male and female artists, and by couples who, together, come close to Virginia Woolf's concept of androgyny.

The titles of all six novels point to the crucial role of the female in conveying Bouraoui's transcultural vision. *Bangkok Blues* might seem to be a possible exception, but one "sings the blues" for suffering in love. The original title of *Bangkok Blues*, moreover, was *Lunaison*, a neologism suggesting the ephemeral nature of the "liaison" of Koï and Virgulius. Koï thai, a modern woman of the Far East, opens the eyes of the Maghrebian Virgulius (Maghreb means the West according to Eastern and Middle Eastern perceptions) to an ancient past which is alien to him. She accomplishes this, however, largely by her silence, the gaps in her speech, and above all by the symbolism associating her with the hand, the khamsa, which in the Maghreb wards off the evil eye.

Retour à Thyna seems to name a place, not a woman, but Thyna, the Roman Thaenae, becomes identified with the heroine, Zitouna, whose name, signifying olive/olive tree, also, in its last two syllables, evokes/ sounds like Thyna. Zitouna's mission, moreover, is to bring ancient Thyna back into the womb of the mother, the Médina. An amateur (lover of) archaeologist, she also promotes the dead Kateb's work, and assumes the function of talespinner in the marketplace.

La Pharaone was originally entitled *Nilamourir*, again a neologism equating the Nile ("Nihil," suggests François Bruzzo 9) with « amour » and « mort ». the love/death theme which has haunted literature from the beginning of time (see Denis de Rougemont, *Love in the Western World*). As is the case with *Lunaison*, the original title underlines the role of the couple. But *La Pharaone*, the final title, sends the reader in the direction of the female characters, the modern Moslem Egyptian Imane, the Frenchwoman Francine, the Canadian Margaret and her daughter Betty, and the ancient Hatchepsut, the female Pharaoh, who dared to adopt male attributes to consolidate her power, a power to promote, above all, peace, justice, and tolerance: "Make love, not war."

In *Ainsi parle la Tour CN*, we encounter two heroines, one apparently inanimate, the CN Tower in Toronto, which only discovers its female identity in the course of the novel, and the other, the mystical Amerindian Twylla Blue, who brings the totemic Moose-Spirit, the « Esprit-Orignal », to "impregnate" the Tower with values of nature and the acceptance of difference. The love of man and woman expands outwards, as a stone thrown into water creates wider and wider concentric circles. The Tower, finally, is in love with all the characters who enter and leave her, especially the First Nations and the recent immigrants, the marginalized in Canadian society.

The title of *La Composée* signifies a woman, Héloïse, who turns out by the end of the novel to be more the "composer" than the "composition." Architect, painter, scholar, finally the author of her own story in epistolary form, Héloïse, like Hatchepsut, assumes the right to speak only at the end of the novel. In so doing, she shatters all of Samir's misperceptions and misconceptions, and he is left with only the "Black Box" of his crash.

La Femme d'entre les lignes foregrounds the female role, that of Lisa/Palimpseste, but she is to be read only "between the lines," subtended, to be decoded by the artist/protagonist and the reader/detective. In some ways this novel presents the opposite side of the coin of the female role: a heroine, Lisa, who is given to self-surrender, complete immersion in her artist (hero? lover?) – or, perhaps, in his work, an ambiguity which torments the narrator. But, as in *La Composée*, there is a sting in the tail of this text: the Muse, Lisa, chooses to disappear and is replaced by the more combative, aggressive Palimpseste, who confronts and confounds the narrator. In effect, again, the Muse strikes back.

Not only do these women assume the right to speak – in Zitouna's case, in a very public performance – they seize love just as they do language. Not for them the "biological tradeoff" implied by Virginia Woolf's *A Room of One's Own* (1929) in which women either produce babies or books. With the possible exception of Lisa, none of these women fear commitment, including Twylla's to the Malaysian Zinal, and Hatchepsut's to her scribe/architect Senmut/Kabar. But even Lisa/Palimpseste seems to question not her own commitment, but the narrator's lack of it.

Love does not, however, prevent these women from critiquing, even at times satirizing, the male point of view. If Koï restricts herself to correcting Virgulius by her silences, the other female protagonists assume a more active role. Zitouna is, more than anyone, aware of Kateb's debauchery, though there was no doubt of her reluctant attraction to him. The shy Mansour becomes the love of her life, but she is conscious that she needs to take the lead in their relationship.

In *La Pharaone*, Francine waxes sarcastic about Barka's fixation on the long-dead Queen. But when he follows Hatchepsut in death, it is Francine who pieces together his fragmentary notes, with the aid of Imane, including transcriptions of Hatchepsut's tablets. Francine transcends sexual jealousy – as Hatchepsut at a crucial moment could not – to the point that the Frenchwoman *becomes* her imagined rival.

Turning 360 degrees in one hour, the CN Tower strives for a balanced view of all her characters, showing special sympathy for the Amerindians, Pete Deloon, Twylla Blue, and Moki, and for the recent immigrants, Souleyman the African and Symphorien, the half-mad poetic Frenchman. The two French Canadians *de souche*, Marc Durocher and Marcel-Marie Duboucher, while in the final analysis dangerous, are treated for the most part like comic relief. The least sympathetic character, from the Tower's point of view, is Kelly King, who is at the controls and has inherited the power and the racism of impervious old Anglo-Canada. Like Francine in *La Pharaone*, Twylla transcends sexual jealousy – Kelly, as sexual predator, has seduced her husband Pete – to become a mentor to Kelly.

With Héloïse, in *La Composée*, we reach a kind of apotheosis of the heroine as artist. The most powerful character in the novel, she is, like Koï thai, silent for the first fifty-odd pages, but she comes into her own with a vengeance. As multi-talented artist and principal speaker, she repudiates all the male voices recounting her tale, particularly those of Jean-Marc Léger and Samir Arhab, to tell her own story, valorizing only the father she has herself chosen, Ali Ben Mokhtar, the old writer.

Lisa/Palimpseste, in *La Femme d'entre les lignes*, seems at first antithetical to Zitouna, Hatchepsut/Francine, Héloïse. Worshipful in the extreme, almost sycophantic, she turns on her putative "creator" at last (perhaps alerted by the sad fate of her only serious predecessor Rose), steps down from the pedestal, and refuses the passive role of Muse. The psychological violence of this text produces a sharp concussion in both narrator and reader, leading to a "shock of recognition" that to ignore the female principle is to cripple, even paralyze art, and to falsify human history. For woman must and will emerge (as in Homer's day) from "between the lines."

All of Bouraoui's novels have completely open endings, inviting us to speculate beyond the last page. But each new novel sets off on a different voyage into space and time, crossing cultures and genders/genres. His entire *œuvre* to date should be regarded as a "work in progress". We await his next lyric novels to learn our new temporal and spatial destinations, and the roles of male and female artists in exploring the trajectory.

Bibliography

Primary texts

Bouraoui, Hédi. *Ainsi Parle la Tour CN.* Tunis : Les Éditions L'Or du Temps, and Vanier, Ontario : Les Éditions L'Interligne, Collection « Vertiges », 1999.

______. *Bangkok Blues.* Ottawa : Vermillon, 1994.

______. *La Composée.* Vanier : Les Éditions L'Interligne, 2001.

______. *La femme d'entre les lignes.* Toronto : Les Éditions du Gref, 2002.

______. *La Pharaone.* Tunis : Les Éditions L'Or du Temps, 1998.

______. *Retour à Thyna.* Tunis : Les Éditions L'Or du Temps, 1996 ; second edition, 1997.

Other works cited

"Actualités littéraires de la francophonie nord-américaine (à l'exception du Québec)." *Études francophones* (Louisiana) 17:2 (automne 2002): 143.

A.D. "*Retour à Thyna* de Hédi Bouraoui." *La Presse:* "Cultures" (samedi 13 juillet 1996): 13.

Belaïd, Mohamed Majdi. "Rencontre avec Monsieur Hédi Bouraoui et discussion autour du *Retour à Thyna.*" *La Gazette du Sud* (janvier 1997): 28-29.

______. "*Retour à Thyna* ou la mémoire restituée." *La Gazette du Sud* (avril 1996): 34-35.

______. "*Retour à Thyna* est un jalon historique auquel on peut se référer." *La Gazette du Sud* (août 1996): 16, 18.

Bélanger, Georges. "Zarathoustra ou La Super Tour: 'Chercher le langage qui réconcilie'." *Liaison* 106 (n.d.): 31-2.

Bélanger, Louis. "Trois Récits d'ailleurs." *Liaison* 98: 39, 41.

Ben Amor, Sadok. "Hédi Bouraoui et la tour CN." *Alfa* 36 (mars 2001): n.p.

Ben Ouanes, Kamel. "*La Pharaone* de Hédi Bouraoui: Fresque romanesque et esthétique hybride." *Le Temps* (mercredi 23 décembre 1998): 8.

Benzina, Rafik. "Heureux récipiendaires: Prix littéraire et de création culturelle 1995 de la ville de Sfax." *La Presse* (mardi 23 juillet 1996): 12.

Bouaouina, Kamel. "*Retour à Thyna*, de Hédi Bouraoui: L'Identité d'une ville." *Le Temps* (mercredi 31 juillet 1996): 8.

Bouraoui, Hédi. Interview: "Le Prix Christine Dumitriu van-Saanen 2000 à Hédi Bouraoui." *L'Express* (du 17 au 23 octobre 2000): 10.

_______. *The Critical Strategy*. Toronto: ECW, 1983.

_______. *The Canadian Alternative*. Toronto: ECW, 1980.

_______. *Créaculture I, II*. Philadelphia: CCD, and Montréal: Marcel Didier, 1971.

Bourial, Hatem. "Au coude du Nil: le couple." *La Presse littéraire* (le 20 juillet 1998): 10.

_______. "Le Roman tunisien dans tous ses états." *La Presse littéraire* (le 6 juillet 1998): 9.

_______. "Vivre et écrire aux sources du futur : un entretien avec Hédi Bouraoui." *La Presse littéraire* (lundi 29 juillet 1996): 10.

Boussis-Kedous, Sofia. "*La Pharaone* de Hédi Bouraoui." *La Presse* (le 14 juin 1999): 10.

Broucq, Claudette. "*La Pharaone* de Hédi Bouraoui: Le Paradigme du troisième millénaire." *Le Temps littéraire* (le 20 octobre 1999): 8.

_______. "À la gloire de l'olivier." *La Presse littéraire* (le 8 juillet 1996): 12.

Bianchi, Pier Paolo. "Et l'avenir recomposé...". *Art Sud* 34 (avril-mai-juin 2002): n.p.

Bruzzo, François. "Épilogue," *Retour à Thyna.*

_______. "Retour aux sources fondatrices d'un écrivain se scrutant en son origine." *Le Temps* (le 14 juin 2000): 9.

Cather, Willa. *My Antonia*. Boston: Houghton Mifflin, 1949 (orig. 1918).

Chagraoui, Mohamed. "*Ainsi parle la Tour CN:* roman de Hédi Bouraoui." *Le Temps* (le 15 février 2000): 16.

_______. "Droit à la différence et à la dignité." *Le Renouveau* (le 20 janvier 1999): n.p.

Chammam, Dorra. "Hédi Bouraoui et *la Pharaone*." *Le Renouveau* (le 9 juillet 1998): 13.

_______. "*Retour à Thyna:* Zitouna aux portes, clés de la mémoire." *La Gazette du Sud* (février 1998).

Chopin, Kate. *The Awakening*. New York: Norton, 1976 (orig. 1899).

D'Ambrosio, Nicola. "Hédi Bouraoui: *La Composée*." *Rivista di Studi Canadesi* 15 (2002): 196-98.

Desjarlais-Heynneman, Mireille. "Parutions récentes: un quatuor d'auteurs torontois." *L'Express* (du 28 février au 6 mars 1995): 10.

Djedidi, Hafidh. "Amourir." *La Presse* (le 19 octobre 1998): n.p.

_______. "Dire autrement la quête identitaire." *La Presse* (le 5 avril 1999): 8.

_______. "*La Pharaone:* Roman de l'écrivoyance." *La Presse* (le 3 mai 1999): 10.

Elbaz, Robert. *"Bangkok Blues." LittéRéalité* VII: 1-2 (1995): 149-154.

_______. "*Retour à Thyna* ou l'éclatement du roman mémorial." *Hédi Bouraoui: La Transpoésie.* Coordonné par Mansour M'Henni. Tunis: L'Or du Temps, 1997. 141-52.

Eliot, T. S. *The Waste Land and Other Poems*. New York: Harcourt Brace, 1934 (orig. 1922).

Fitzgerald, F. Scott. *The Great Gatsby*. New York: Scribner's, 1953 (orig. 1925).

Fleurant, Kenneth J. "Hédi Bouraoui: *La Pharaone*." *The French Review* 75: 2 (May 2002): 1306-07.

Ghachem, Moncef. "Interstices pharaoniens." *Le Temps* (le 16 décembre 1998): 8.

Girard, René. *Mensonge poétique et vérité romanesque*. Paris: Grasset, 1961.

Guermazi, Jamel. "*Bangkok Blues:* Nouveau-né de Hédi Bouraoui." *Le Temps* (Tunis), 5 avril 1995. Reprinted in *La Toison d'or* (Bergerac) 35 (hiver 1994): 40-41.

Guillery, Catherine. "L'Impression de Catherine Guillery: *La Pharaone.*" 51-2.

James, Henry. "Preface" to *The Portrait of a Lady.* Boston: Houghton Mifflin Riverside Edition, 1956; orig. publ. 1881. 3-15.

Karch, Pierre. "Romans Politico-Sociaux." *University of Toronto Quarterly* 70: 1 (Winter 2000): 12.

_______. "Deux profs, deux romans, deux mythologies personnelles." *Liaison* (mars 1995): 36.

Kateb Yacine. *Nedjma.* Paris: Le Seuil, 1956.

Kéfi, Ridha. "À la recherche d'Hatchepsout." *Jeune Afrique.* Tunis: L'Or du Temps, 1998: 120.

Lawrence, D. H. *Studies in Classic American Literature.* New York: Doubleday, 1951 (orig. 1923).

Léon, Pierre. "Avec un finaliste du prix Trillium, la Tour CN perd la tête." *L'Express* (du 11 au 18 avril 2000): 8.

Maazaoui, Abbes. "Hédi Bouraoui: *La Pharaone.*" *Études Francophones* (Louisiana) XIV: 2. 201-06.

Mahfoudh, Ahmed. "La Quête de l'espace originel dans le roman tunisien des années '90." *IBLA* 60: 180 (1997): 153-61.

Naudillon, Françoise. "Hédi Bouraoui:*Ainsi Parle la Tour CN.*" *Rivista di Studi Canadesi* 13 (2000): 162-64.

_______. "*Retour à Thyna* ou la lucidité du fils prodigue." *Hédi Bouraoui: La Transpoésie.*

_______. "Ifriqiya et la Caraïbe dans l'oeuvre d'Hédi Bouraoui." *Hédi Bouraoui: Iconoclaste et chantre du transculturel,* ed. Jacques Cotnam. Ottawa: Le Nordir, 1996. 43-57.

Price, Reynolds. "Men, Creating Women." The New York *Times Book Review*, November 9, 1986: 1, 16, 18, 20.

Sabiston, Elizabeth. Introduction to Hédi Bouraoui, *Échosmos.* Toronto: Mosaic Press and Canadian Association for the Comparative Study of Civilizations, 1986.

Sauvalle, Daniel. "Hédi Bouraoui: *Retour à Thyna.*" *Jointure* 62 (été 1999): 89-90.

Toso-Rodinis, Juliana. "*Retour à Thyna* de Hédi Bouraoui et ses éléments de romanité." *La Tunisie dans la littérature tunisienne de langue arabe et de langue française: Actes du Colloque dirigé par Habib Salha.* Tunis: L'Or du Temps, 2001. 213-28.

Touraine, Alain. Conference at York University, Toronto, November, 2001. Comments from Hédi Bouraoui.

Triki, Rachida. "Du nomadisme à la matrice natale." *La Presse littéraire* (lundi 8 juillet 1996): 12. Rptd. in *La Gazette du Sud* (août 1996): 18.

Yefsah, Rachid. "Cantos: Un Nomade chez les Thaïlandais." *Jeune Afrique* (23-29 mars 1995): 60.

Young, Lélia. "Hédi Bouraoui: *La Composée.*" *LittéRéalité* (2002): 118.

Printed in
March 2005
at Gauvin Press Ltd., Gatineau, Québec